# Vocabulary in practice 3

Glennis Pye

40 units of self-study vocabulary exercises

with tests

CAMBRIDGE UNIVERSITY PRESS

Published in South Asia by

**Cambridge University Press India Pvt. Ltd.**
CAMBRIDGE HOUSE
4381/4 Ansari Road
Daryaganj, New Delhi 110002


First South Asian Edition 2005
Reprinted 2007, 2009, 2011, 2012 (twice), 2013

ISBN 13: 978-81-7596-249-1
Special edition for sale in South Asia only, not for export elsewhere.



This edition of *Glennis Pye / Vocabulary in Practice 3 & 4* is published by arrangement with Cambridge University Press, The Edinburgh Building, Shaftesbury Road, Cambridge CB2 2RU, UK.

Published by Manas Saikia for Cambridge University Press India Pvt. Ltd and printed & bound at Raj Press, R-3 Inderpuri, New Delhi - 110012

# Contents

# To the student

This book will give you the chance to practise your vocabulary in a fun way.

*Vocabulary in Practice 3* has:

- 40 units of short, enjoyable exercises – each unit practises groups of words which belong together
- 4 Tests – one after every 10 units, helping you to remember the words from those units
- an Answer Key
- a Word List – this is a list of all the words in each unit with information about how the words are used.

You can use the book in two ways:

1 Start at the beginning of the book. Do units 1–40 and then do the Tests.
2 Look at the Contents. Do the units you think are important first. When you have finished the book, do the Tests.

You can do each unit in two ways:

1 Do the unit and check your answers in the Answer Key. Study the Word List and learn the words you got wrong. Then do the exercise again.
2 Study the Word List for the unit. Then do the unit and check your answers.

**Note** Do the exercises in this book in pencil. Then you can do the exercises again after a week or a month. Repeating the exercises will help you to remember the words.

Here are some ideas to help you to learn vocabulary:

- Learn groups of words which belong together [e.g. skirt, coat, trousers, etc.].
- Learn a word and also its opposite [e.g. beautiful/ugly, hot/cold].
- Draw pictures: some words are easier to remember if you draw a picture and write the word under it, e.g.

- Write new words in a notebook: write the meaning in English or in your own language, then write a sentence using the word.

I hope you find this book useful and that it makes learning English words fun.

# 1 The family

## A Complete what the people are saying with the words in the box.

brother-in-law daughter-in-law father-in-law grandparents great-grandfather great-grandmother mother-in-law sister-in-law ~~son-in-law~~ step-brother step-daughter step-father step-mother step-sister step-son

BERNARD: There's me, next to my daughter, Jenny, and that's Paul, my (1) ......son-in-law...... . That's Paul's (2) .................., Jack. He and Paul's mother, Jill, got married last year. And there's Paul's (3) .................., Bob and Sheila. They're Jill's parents.

JILL: There's me, next to my son, Paul, and that's Jenny, my (4) .................. . That's my other son, Jason, and next to him are Simon, my (5) .................., and Beth, my (6) .................. – Jack's children from his first marriage.

JENNY: There's Jill and Jason, my (7) .................. and my (8) .................. . That's Rowena, my (9) .................. . She and Dad got married about three years ago. And there's my (10) .................. and (11) .................., Betty and Harold – they're my grandmother's parents. That's my sister, Faye, standing next to Jason.

PAUL: There's Bernard, my (12) .................., and Faye, my (13) .................. . And that's Beth and Simon, my (14) .................. and (15) .................. .

# 2 People you know

## A Put the words in the box into the correct group.

| ~~acquaintance~~ boss boyfriend classmate close friend colleague friend of the family girlfriend mate neighbour relative |
|---|

| family | school | where you live |
|---|---|---|
| ........................ | ........................ | ........................ |
| **love** | **work** | **other** |
| ........................ | ........................ | ....acquaintance.... |
| ........................ | ........................ | ........................ |
| | | ........................ |
| | | ........................ |

## B Complete the sentences with one of the words on the right.

| | |
|---|---|
| 1 I have lots of ......mates...... , but very few close friends. | classmates / mates |
| 2 He's ........................ , really. I've only met him a few times. | an acquaintance / a close friend |
| 3 She's a good ........................ . She pays me well and is always very fair. | boss / relative |
| 4 I love going to work. My ........................ are great fun. | colleagues / neighbours |
| 5 It's her sixth birthday next week. She's invited her ........................ to tea. | boyfriends / classmates |
| 6 Do you like your new house? Have you met your ........................ yet? | friends of the family / neighbours |
| 7 Our family is quite small, so I haven't got many ........................ . | girlfriends / relatives |
| 8 Amy's got a new ........................ . | boyfriend / relative |
| 9 Jim isn't my uncle, he's just a ........................ . | boss / friend of the family |
| 10 Ian says he's going to ask his ........................ to marry him. | colleague / girlfriend |
| 11 If you have a problem, it helps if you can talk to ........................ about it. | an acquaintance / a close friend |

# 3 Clothes

**A** **Write the clothes words in the box in the correct suitcase.**

| bikini | fleece | sandals | sunglasses | sunhat | swimming costume |
|---|---|---|---|---|---|
| trunks | walking boots | waterproof jacket | | | |

**B** **Label the pictures with the words from A.**

1 ..............................    6 ..............................    8 ..............................
2 ..............................    7 ..............................    9 ..............................
3 ..............................
4 ..............................
5 ..............................

**C** **The underlined words are in the wrong sentences. Write the correct word for each sentence.**

1 You wear underpants on your feet in the house. ........*slippers*........
2 You wear a bra in the house before you get dressed. ..............................
3 A woman wears slippers under her trousers. ..............................
4 A woman wears a vest in bed. ..............................
5 A man wears pyjamas under his trousers. ..............................
6 A woman wears a dressing gown under her blouse. ..............................
7 A man wears knickers in bed. ..............................
8 You wear a nightie under your jumper. ..............................

# 4 Clothes and accessories

## A Complete the sentences with the words in the box.

belt bracelet comb earrings ~~lipstick~~
necklace purse ring shoelaces wallet

1 One of the women isn't wearing lipstick .

2 One of the women isn't wearing .................................. .

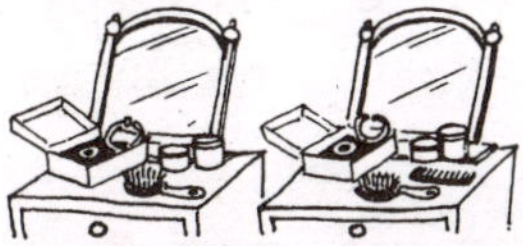

3 One of the dressing tables hasn't got a .................................. on it.

4 One of the men hasn't got a .................................. .

5 One of the women isn't wearing a .................................. .

6 One of the pairs of shoes hasn't got any .................................. .

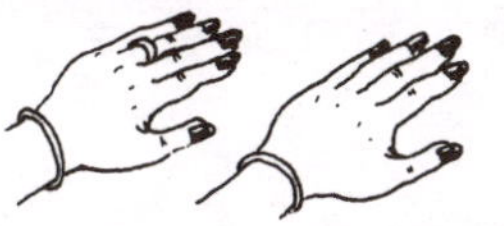

7 One of the women isn't wearing a .................................. .

8 One of the dolls isn't wearing a .................................. .

9 One of the bags doesn't have a .................................. .

10 One of the shops hasn't got a .................................. .

# 5 Life

**A** **Look at the pictures and complete the sentences with the words in the box.**

1

2

3

4

5

6

7

8

9

10

11

12

| died | fell in love | got divorced | got engaged | got married |
|---|---|---|---|---|
| grew up | had a baby | moved house | retired | started school |
| was born | went to university | | | |

1 Jack .................................... in the country.

2 When he was two years old, his parents .................................... .

3 So Jack .................................... in the city.

4 When he was five years old, Jack .................................... .

5 At the age of eighteen, he .................................... .

6 He met Jenny there and .................................... .

7 They .................................... immediately.

8 When they finished university, they .................................... .

9 Soon they .................................... and were happy for many years.

10 When Jack .................................... , he and Jenny began to argue.

11 A few years later, they .................................... .

12 Not long after that, Jack .................................... .

# 6 Describing character

**A Put the words in the box into the correct group.**

| generous | impatient | lovely | mean | patient |
|---|---|---|---|---|
| polite | rude | selfish | sensible | silly |

**bad qualities:** ........................................

**good qualities:** ........................................

**B Match the sentences on the left with the replies on the right. Write the letters in the box below.**

1 She wants to give me some money as a gift.
2 She just walked straight past without even saying hello.
3 She always says please and thank you.
4 She hates waiting for anything. She wants everything to be done right now.
5 She's very good with the children. I never worry about them when she's there.
6 I really like Rich's new girlfriend.
7 She only thinks about herself.
8 She never gets angry, even when she has to explain things to them again and again.
9 She's always telling jokes and playing tricks on people.
10 He asked if he could use her car to get to the hospital, but she just said no.

a Oh, she's so rude.
b I know, she's very sensible, isn't she?
c I know, she's so selfish, isn't she?
d Yes, she's a very polite girl.
e Yes, she seems lovely, doesn't she?
f I know, she's so impatient, isn't she?
g Oh, she's so mean.
h I think she's too silly sometimes, don't you?
i Yes, she's really patient, isn't she?
j She's always so generous, isn't she?

| | | | | |
|---|---|---|---|---|
| 1 ........ | 2 ........ | 3 ........ | 4 ........ | 5 ........ |
| 6 ........ | 7 ........ | 8 ........ | 9 ........ | 10 ........ |

# 7 Describing appearance

**A** **Find twelve adjectives for describing appearance in the grid. Then complete the words in the list below.**

| d | a | r | k | - | s | k | i | n | n | e | d | p |
|---|---|---|---|---|---|---|---|---|---|---|---|---|
| i | n | c | k | o | l | p | l | o | a | l | w | l |
| n | s | o | n | i | i | g | o | v | n | b | e | a |
| d | c | u | t | e | m | p | r | e | t | t | y | i |
| t | r | e | n | d | y | r | u | r | q | u | e | n |
| r | u | o | c | h | i | n | d | w | h | l | t | x |
| y | f | d | i | n | c | h | o | e | w | p | h | o |
| v | f | a | i | r | - | s | k | i | n | n | e | d |
| o | y | t | z | i | e | l | e | g | a | n | t | o |
| p | j | l | q | u | h | s | g | h | b | e | c | h |
| y | i | a | u | s | m | a | r | t | m | r | a | m |
| t | g | o | o | d | - | l | o | o | k | i | n | g |

1 c _ _ _
2 d _ _ _ - _ _ _ _ _ _ _
3 e _ _ _ _ _ _ _
4 f _ _ _ - _ _ _ _ _ _ _
5 g _ _ _ - _ _ _ _ _ _ _
6 o _ _ _ _ _ _ _ _ _ _
7 p _ _ _ _
8 p _ _ _ _ _
9 s _ _ _ _ _ _
10 s _ _ _
11 s _ _ _ _
12 t _ _ _ _ _

**B** **Complete what the people are saying with the words from A.**

1 Jane's new boyfriend looks like a model. He's very .................................... .
2 If you're going for an interview, you'd better make sure you look .................................... .
3 I'm a bit .................................... . I need to go on a diet.
4 I'm .................................... , so I try to keep out of the sun completely.
5 Oh look! She's so .................................... . How many months old is she?
6 She isn't beautiful, but she isn't ugly either. She's just .................................... .
7 You still have to be careful in the sun even if you're .................................... .
8 He looks really .................................... in his designer clothes.
9 I always look so .................................... . I really need to buy some new clothes.
10 Penny's got a lovely face and beautiful hair. She's very .................................... .
11 I want to be .................................... , but I just don't seem to be able to lose weight.
12 I'm so short. I could never look .................................... .

# 8 How you feel

## A Circle the correct word for each picture.

1

cheerful / embarrassed

2

relaxed / worried

3

jealous / pleased

4

annoyed / guilty

5

miserable / proud

6

fed up / surprised

## B Complete the sentences with the other words from A.

1 I have no job, no money and I can't sleep at night – I feel so miserable .

2 People think I'm .................... because she's got a boyfriend and I haven't.

3 I feel .................... about not visiting my grandmother in hospital.

4 I'm not .................... they're getting married – they've known each other a long time.

5 I'm .................... about you walking home on your own at night.

6 And then I just started to cry in front of everyone – I felt so .................... .

# 9 Having a bad day

## A Match the words and expressions on the left with the definitions on the right. Write the letters in the box below.

1 run out of
2 oversleep
3 have an argument
4 break down
5 fall over
6 miss
7 get lost
8 be late
9 be stuck in a traffic jam
10 spill

a fall to the ground
b be in a line of cars that is not moving
c not get up early enough
d arrive too late to get on a vehicle
e not be able to find your way
f stop working
g make liquid pour somewhere by mistake
h not have any of something left
i arrive after the correct time
j talk angrily with someone

| 1 ........ | 2 ........ | 3 ........ | 4 ........ | 5 ........ |
|---|---|---|---|---|
| 6 ........ | 7 ........ | 8 ........ | 9 ........ | 10 ........ |

## B Complete the paragraph with the expressions from A. Remember to write the verbs in the past tense.

I had a very bad day yesterday. I usually get up at seven o'clock, but I (1) ...overslept... and didn't get up until eight. Then I (2) .................... the bus and had to wait twenty minutes for the next one to come. Of course I (3) .................... for work and I could see my boss wasn't very pleased. The rest of the morning was OK, but as I was walking to the staff restaurant for lunch, I (4) .................... and hurt my wrist. I was really happy when it was time to go home. But things didn't get any better, I'm afraid. There was a new driver on the bus. He went the wrong way and (5) .................... . He turned into a very busy road and we (6) .................... for about twenty minutes. Then the bus (7) .................... petrol and (8) .................... . I had to get off and walk the rest of the way home. When I got home, I decided to relax with a nice cup of tea, but I (9) .................... it all over my new skirt. I phoned my boyfriend, thinking he would make me feel better, but he said something unkind about one of my friends and we (10) .................... . I hope today is going to be better.

# 10 Accidents and injuries

## A Complete the sentences on the left with the words in the box. Then match the sentences on the left with the reasons on the right. Write the letters in the box below.

black   broken   bruise   burn   cut   ~~swollen~~

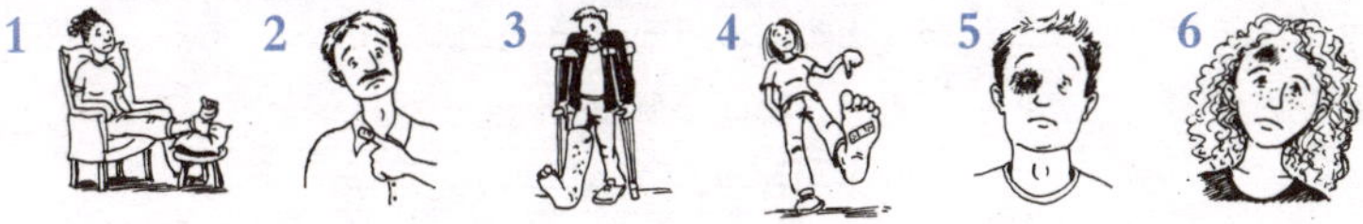

| | |
|---|---|
| **1** I've got a ....swollen.... ankle. | **a** I got into a fight. |
| **2** I've got a .................... on my finger. | **b** I fell off my motorbike. |
| **3** I've got a .................... leg. | **c** I touched a hot iron. |
| **4** I've got a nasty .................... on my foot. | **d** I slipped while I was out running. |
| **5** I've got a .................... eye. | **e** I walked into a door. |
| **6** I've got an enormous .................... on my forehead. | **f** I stood on some broken glass. |

**1** ...d... **2** ........ **3** ........ **4** ........ **5** ........ **6** ........

## B Complete the dialogue with the words in the box.

bandage   bleeding   had an accident   hurt   injured
pain   stitches   treatment   unconscious

Amy: Did you hear? Marcia's (1) .................... . She fell off her bike and landed on her head. She was (2) .................... for about ten minutes. When she woke up, she didn't know where she was.

Kate: Was she badly (3) .................... ?

Amy: Well, her head was (4) .................... and she was in a lot of (5) .................... .

Kate: What (6) .................... did she need?

Amy: She needed a few (7) .................... in her head – she said having them put in (8) .................... more than anything. She's also got a (9) .................... around her wrist.

# Test 1 (Units 1–10)

**A Complete the sentences with words for the people in your family and people you know.**

1 This is my ........................................., Ben. My husband's brother.
2 This is my ........................................., Jackie. We sit next to each other at work.
3 This is my ........................................., Hugh. He lives next door.
4 This is my ........................................., Angela. My wife's mother.
5 This is my ........................................., Kath. My dad's new wife.
6 This is my ......................................... . My mum's granddad.
7 This is my ........................................., David. I've worked for him for three years.
8 This is my ........................................., Max. He's my husband's son from his first marriage.

**B Match the words in the box with Gemma and Sarah's appearance. Then write lists of what the girls are wearing.**

| overweight plain pretty scruffy slim smart |
|---|

**Gemma** **appearance** **Sarah**

..................................... .....................................
..................................... .....................................
..................................... .....................................

**clothes and accessories**

..................................... .....................................
..................................... .....................................
..................................... .....................................
..................................... .....................................
.....................................
.....................................
.....................................

# Test 1 (Units 1–10)

**C When do we usually do these things in our life? Put the words in the box in the correct order.**

be born   die   fall in love   get engaged   get married
have a baby   retire   start school

1 ................ 2 ................ 3 ................ 4 ................
5 ................ 6 ................ 7 ................ 8 ................

**D What are the people like? Match the words in the box with what they are saying.**

generous   impatient   selfish   sensible   silly   rude

1 Have my chocolate – I can get some more. ................
2 I don't care about them – I've got my own problems. ................
3 Let's put jam all around his mouth while he's asleep! ................
4 Come on, hurry up! I can't wait any longer! ................
5 Move! That's my chair. ................
6 Let's cross the road at the zebra crossing. It's safer there. ................

**E Complete the sentences with one word or expression from each box. Remember to put the verbs in the correct form.**

annoyed   embarrassed
guilty   miserable
pleased   worried

be late   fall over   have an accident
have an argument   not be in pain   spill

1 She's ................ because she ................ with her boyfriend last night.
2 She's ................ because she ................ in front of the whole class.
3 She's ................ because he ................ coffee all over her carpet.
4 She feels ................ because she hasn't visited a friend who ................ last week.
5 She's ................ because he ................ and she thinks they're going to miss their train.
6 She's ................ because the drugs worked and she ................ any more.

# 11 Shops and shopping

## A Label the pictures with the words in the box.

baker's basket butcher's checkout chemist's clothes shop trolley
department store gift shop hairdresser's newsagent's supermarket

1 ..........................

2 ..........................

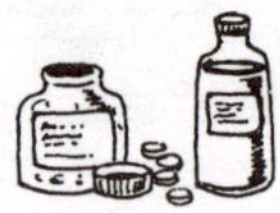

3 ..........................

4 ..........................

5 ..........................

6 ..........................

7 ..........................

8 ..........................

9 ..........................

10 ..........................

11 ..........................

12 ..........................

## B Complete the paragraph with the words in the box.

changing room cost fit pay receipt shop assistant till try on

At the weekend I went shopping for a new pair of jeans. There were so many different types, I didn't know which ones to choose. A (1) .......................... came over and asked me if I needed any help. 'Why don't you (2) .......................... a few pairs?' she suggested.

'Good idea,' I replied. 'Then I can see if they (3) .......................... me.'

'There's a (4) .......................... just over there,' she said.

After deciding which pair I liked best, I checked the label to see how much they (5) .......................... . They were quite cheap so I decided to buy two pairs. I took them to the man at the (6) .......................... .

'Can I (7) .......................... by cheque or credit card?' I asked.

'Yes, of course,' he replied. 'Would you like me to put your (8) .......................... in the bag? You should keep it in case you want to bring them back.'

# 12 Houses and homes

## A Match the people with their homes.

- I live in a bungalow. ☐
- I live in a house. 1
- I live in a flat. ☐
- I live in a cottage. ☐

## B Label the pictures with the words in the box.

| block of | detached | semi-detached | terraced |
|---|---|---|---|

1 .................................... house

2 .................................... flats

3 .................................... houses

4 .................................... houses

## C Look at the picture and complete the sentences with the words in the box.

| basement | first floor | ground floor | second floor |
|---|---|---|---|

1 Jamie is spending £95,000.
He's buying the .................................... flat.

2 Laura is spending £85,000.
She's buying the .................................... flat.

3 Helena is spending £110,000.
She's buying the .................................... flat.

4 Marc is spending £70,000.
He's buying the .................................... flat.

# 13 Housework

## A Label the pictures with the words in the box.

dishwasher dustbin duster iron ironing board pegs
vacuum cleaner washing line washing machine

1 ..............................
2 ..............................
3 ..............................
4 ..............................
5 ..............................
6 ..............................
7 ..............................
8 ..............................
9 ..............................

## B What do you use when you need to do these jobs around the house? Put the words from A into the correct group.

**do the dishes**

..............................

**do the ironing**

..............................

..............................

**do the washing**

..............................

..............................

..............................

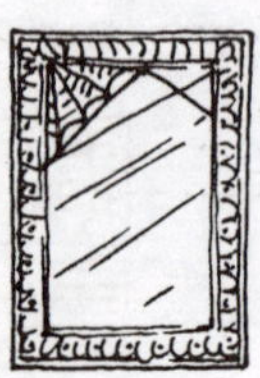

**dust**

..............................

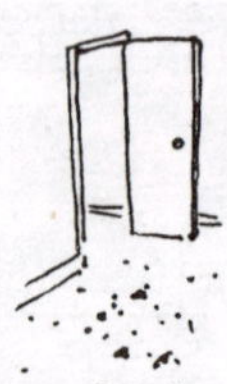

**hoover**

..............................

**put the rubbish out**

..............................

# 14 In the kitchen

## A Label the pictures with the words in the box.

bottle opener   coffee maker   corkscrew   food processor   frying pan
mug   pan   tap   teapot   tea towel   tin opener   washing-up liquid

1 ..................................................

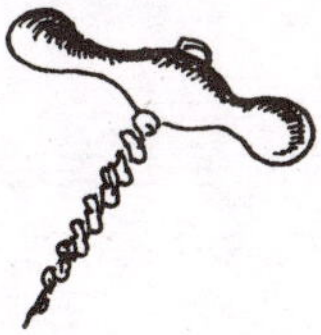

2 ..................................................

3 ..................................................

4 ..................................................

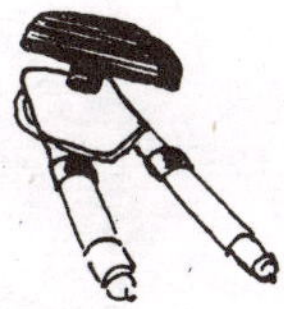

5 ..................................................

6 ..................................................

7 ..................................................

8 ..................................................

9 ..................................................

10 ..................................................

11 ..................................................

12 ..................................................

## B Put the words from A into the correct group.

| for cleaning | for opening things | for drinks | for cooking |
|---|---|---|---|
| .................... | .................... | .................... | .................... |
| .................... | .................... | .................... | .................... |
| .................... | .................... | .................... | .................... |

# 15 Food

**A Tick the eight items Gary has already put in the shopping trolley.**

aubergine ..........
bacon ..........
bread rolls ....✓....
cereal ..........
cheese ..........
cucumber ..........
dried fruit ..........
eggs ..........
frozen vegetables ..........
melon ..........
red pepper ..........
pineapple ..........
sausages ..........
tinned fruit ..........

**B Label the pictures with the other words from A.**

1 ..............................

2 ..............................

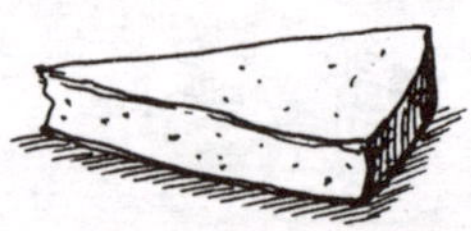

3 ..............................

4 ..............................

5 ..............................

6 ..............................

# 16 Health and fitness

## A Match the words in the box with the definitions.

| be bad for you | be good for you | exercise | fit | ~~healthy~~ | healthy diet |
|---|---|---|---|---|---|
| keep fit | lose weight | put on weight | unfit | unhealthy | |

1 physically strong and not likely to get ill ........healthy........
2 physically strong because you do enough exercise ................
3 to become thinner ................
4 to be good for your health ................
5 physical activity that you do to make your body strong and healthy ................
6 to stay healthy ................
7 to be likely to damage your health ................
8 not physically strong because you do not do enough exercise ................
9 food that is good for your health ................
10 to become fatter ................
11 to not be good for your health ................

## B Complete the paragraph with the words from A. Remember to put the verbs in the correct form.

### Health and fitness

Do you feel good? Are you (1) ....fit.... and (2) ................ ? Maybe you think you are too fat and need to (3) ................ . Or maybe you are too thin and need to (4) ................ . Here is some advice for you. First of all, it is important not to do things that are (5) ................ – so, give up smoking or try to smoke less, do not drink too much alcohol or go to bed too late. If you have an (6) ................ lifestyle, try to change some of the things you do – do things that are (7) ................ . Make sure you eat a (8) ................ , including plenty of fresh fruit and vegetables. Do plenty of (9) ................ to (10) ................ – go running or join your local gym. If you are very (11) ................ , though, you should start with just a little swimming.

# 17 Sport

## A Where do you do these sports? Match the sports with the places.

court ☐

track ☐

pitch ☐

1

2

3

## B Complete the paragraphs about the sports in A with the words in the box. You can use some of the words more than once. Remember to put the verbs in the correct form.

| game | goal | lose | match | player | point | race | score | team | win |
|---|---|---|---|---|---|---|---|---|---|

He's practising for tomorrow's football (1) .................................... . He's a very good (2) .................................... . He hopes he'll (3) .................................... a (4) .................................... and help his (5) .................................... to (6) .................................... . He won't be happy if they (7) .................................... .

She's playing a (8) .................................... of tennis. She's just (9) .................................... a (10) .................................... and needs only one more to (11) .................................... . She's quite a good tennis (12) .................................... .

He's running so fast – I think he's going to (13) .................................... the (14) .................................... .

# 18 Music

## A Put the words in the box into the correct group.

band choir classical music composer conductor jazz
opera orchestra pop music pop star singer

| types of music | people | |
|---|---|---|
| .................... | .................... | .................... |
| .................... | .................... | .................... |
| .................... | .................... | .................... |
| .................... | .................... | .................... |

## B Match the people with the type of music they like.

I like opera. ☐

I like classical music. ☐

I like jazz. ☐

I like pop music. ☐

## C Complete what the people are saying with the words for people from A.

JONATHAN: Last night I saw the opera Don Giovanni. The (1) .................... who was Don Giovanni had a fantastic voice. The music was wonderful too, and the (2) .................... controlled the (3) .................... very well.

BEN: I love classical music and I sing in a small (4) .................... . Next week we're giving a concert of 18th century music by the (5) .................... Mozart.

CHARLOTTE: My young cousin loves pop music. She's a member of a (6) .................... and wants to become a famous (7) .................... .

# 19 Shapes

**A** **Look at the picture. Then complete the answers with the words in the box. Remember to use the plural form if you need to.**

| circle | diamond | heart | oval |
|---|---|---|---|
| rectangle | square | star | triangle |

1 What shape is the car? It's a ......star...... .
2 What shape is the clock face? It's a .................... .
3 What shape is the door of the house? It's a .................... .
4 What shape are the windows of the house? They're .................... .
5 What shape is the sun? It's a .................... .
6 What shape are the wheels on the bicycle? They're .................... .
7 What shape is the cat's body? It's a .................... .
8 What shape are the windows of the church? They're .................... .
9 What shape is the chimney on the house? It's a .................... .
10 What shape are the cat's ears? They're .................... .
11 What shape is the roof of the house? It's a .................... .
12 What shape are the wheels on the car? They're .................... .

**B** **Complete the sentences about the picture in A with the words in the box.**

| circular | diamond-shaped | heart-shaped | oval |
|---|---|---|---|
| rectangular | square | star-shaped | triangular |

1 It's a .................... house with four .................... windows, a .................... door and a .................... roof.
2 It's a .................... car with .................... wheels.
3 It's a bike with .................... wheels.
4 It's a cat with an .................... body and .................... ears.
5 It's a church with .................... windows.

# 20 Measurements

**A Complete the measurements with the words in the box.**

| depth height length weight width |
|---|

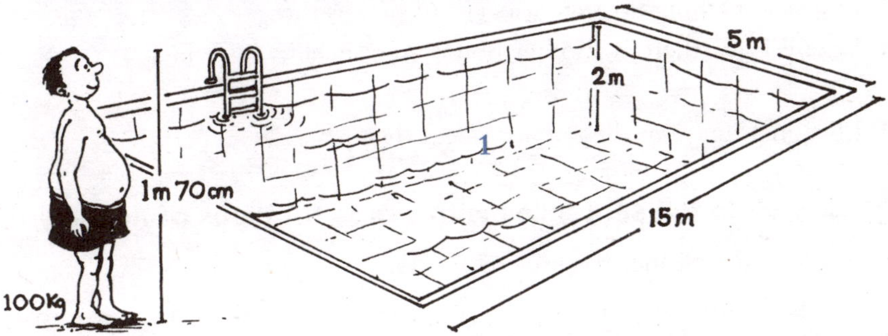


**swimming pool**

1 .................................... 15m
2 .................................... 5m
3 .................................... 2m

**man**

1 .................................... 1m 70cm
2 .................................... 100kg

**B Complete the questions about the items below with the words in the box.**

| deep heavy high long tall weigh wide |
|---|

1 How .................................... is it?
2 How .................................... is it?
3 How .................................... is it?
4 How .................................... is it?
5 How .................................... is she?
6 How .................................... is it?
7 How much does he .................................... ?

# Test 2 (Units 11–20)

## A Complete the sentences with words for shops or houses.

1 I need to buy a newspaper. Is there a .................................... around here?
2 I need something for my headache. Where is the .................................... ?
3 Where I live, there is another house on each side. I live in a
.................................... house.
4 I live in a house in the countryside. I live in a .................................... .

## B Complete the sentences with words for types of housework.

1 The vacuum cleaner has broken, so I can't .................................... .
2 The dishwasher has broken, so I can't do the .................................... .
3 The iron has broken, so I can't do the .................................... .
4 I haven't got a duster, so I can't .................................... .

## C The <u>underlined</u> words are in the wrong sentences. Write the correct word for each sentence.

1 Can you dry the cups for me? The <u>teapot</u> is over there. ....................................
2 I'll open this bottle of wine. Could you pass me the <u>tin opener</u>? ....................................
3 To make fried eggs, first get the <u>tea towel</u> really hot. ....................................
4 Have a beer. Here's the <u>frying pan</u>. ....................................
5 It's a small <u>corkscrew</u>, so you can only make two cups of tea. ....................................
6 I need a <u>bottle opener</u> to open this tin. ....................................

## D Find the first letter and write the words for the foods.

1 small round objects we get from a chicken (g e s g)

....................................

2 meat from a pig cut into thin slices (c a b n o)

....................................

3 solid food made from milk (h c e s e e)

....................................

4 meat pressed into a long tube shape (s u a s s e g a)

....................................

# Test 2 (Units 11–20)

## E Complete what the people are saying.

1 I'm so .................................. . I really don't do enough exercise.

2 Let's have a .................................. – to see who can run the fastest.

3 I like to eat .................................. food – lots of fresh fruit and vegetables.

4 They were lucky. They .................................. a goal in the last minute.

## F Follow the lines. Then complete the sentences.

1 He's in a .............................. band.

2 He's a member of an .............................. .

3 He's a member of a .............................. .

4 He's a .............................. .

## G Follow the instructions and draw the shapes.

Draw a big circle. In the middle of the circle draw a small triangle. Under the triangle draw a rectangle. Above the triangle draw two small ovals. Inside each oval draw a diamond.

## H Complete the sentences with words for measurement.

1 What's the .............................. of this piece of wood? — It's 3m long.

2 How .............................. is this box? — It weighs 3.5kg.

3 What's the .............................. of this room? — It's 3m wide.

4 How .............................. are you? — I'm 1m 67cm.

# 21 Jobs

## A Look at the table and complete the answers with the words in the box.

| | things done in job | hours worked |
|---|---|---|
| **Janice** | dusts, hoovers, irons, etc. | 3 afternoons/week |
| **Eric** | takes photos | 5 days/week |
| **Lena** | keeps records of money for a company | 3 days/week |
| **Tim** | works for the government | 5 days/week |
| **Michelle** | writes instructions for computers | 5 days/week |

an accountant   a civil servant   a cleaner
a computer programmer   a photographer

1 What does Janice do?   She's .................................................. .
2 What does Eric do?   He's .................................................. .
3 What does Lena do?   She's .................................................. .
4 What does Tim do?   He's .................................................. .
5 What does Michelle do?   She's .................................................. .

## B Look at the table in A again. Complete the sentences with the names of the people from A.

1 .......Eric......... , ........................ and ........................ work full-time.
2 ........................ and ........................ work part-time.

## C Complete the advertisements with the words in the box.

au pair   journalist   model   shop assistant

1 **WANTED** ..................................
to write news stories for local newspaper.

2 **WANTED** ..................................
to work at the London Fashion Show. Must be tall, thin and beautiful.

3 **WANTED** ..................................
to look after two children aged 5 and 8. Must speak good English.

4 **WANTED** ..................................
to sell clothing in busy department store. Must be smart and polite.

# 22 In the office

## A Label the picture with the words in the box.

calculator desk tidy diary file filing cabinet
hole punch in-tray/out-tray notepad paper clip
Post-it™ note ring binder stapler

1 ..............................
2 ..............................
3 ..............................
4 ..............................
5 ..............................
6 ..............................
7 ..............................
8 ..............................
9 ..............................
10 ..............................
11 ..............................
12 ..............................

## B Complete the sentences with words from A.

1 Have you got a .............................. ? I need to fasten these pages together, but I don't want to make a hole in them.

2 Have you got a .............................. ? I want to fasten these pages together.

3 There are pens, pencils, rubbers and all sorts of things all over my desk. I need a .............................. .

4 Don't worry, I won't forget. I'll write 'meet Sandy at 2 o'clock' on a .............................. and stick it on my computer.

5 Take a .............................. to the meeting so that you can write down the things you need to remember.

6 I have this .............................. to write down the days and times I have to do things.

# 23 Writing to people

## A The <u>underlined</u> words are in the wrong sentences. Write the correct word for each sentence.

1 The boss sent us <u>a fax</u>, reminding us that we should dress smartly for work. ........................

2 Paul wrote Jenny <u>a postcard</u> explaining why he didn't want to see her any more. ........................

3 We're going on holiday next week – we'll send you <u>a memo</u>. ........................

4 Use your computer and send him <u>a note</u> – it's the quickest way of contacting someone. ........................

5 Mum left me <u>an email</u> asking me to buy milk and bread. ........................

6 Can you send <u>a text message</u>? That'll be quick and we'll have a copy of your order. ........................

7 I've got a mobile phone, but I don't know how to send <u>a letter</u> on it. ........................

## B Label the picture with the words in the box.

| address | envelope | postcode | stamp | writing paper |
|---|---|---|---|---|

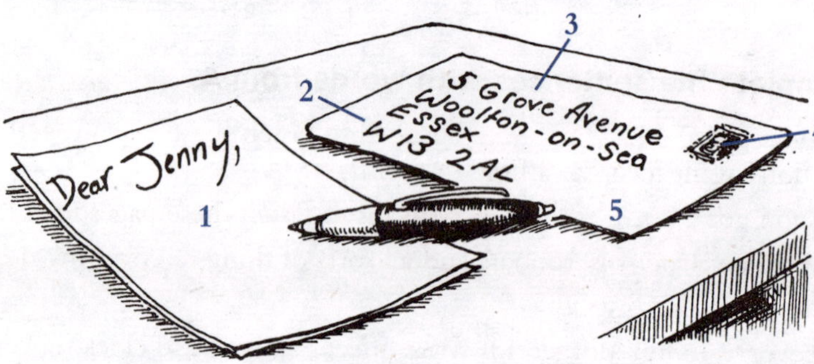


1 ........................

2 ........................

3 ........................

4 ........................

5 ........................

# 24 Holidays

## A Complete the sentences with the words in the box.

| beach holiday | camping holiday | cruise | skiing holiday | walking holiday |
|---|---|---|---|---|

1 I love sleeping outside. I'm going on a ........................................ .

2 I love lying in the sun. I'm going on a ........................................ .

3 I love the mountains in the summer. I'm going on a ................................ .

4 I love the mountains in the winter. I'm going on a ................................ .

5 I love the sea. I'm going on a ........................................ .

## B Complete the sentences with the words in the box.

| bed and breakfast | hotels | tent | villas | youth hostel |
|---|---|---|---|---|

**PANNE ISLAND.** *Where to stay.*

If you like to be comfortable in a place where everything is done for you, there are several excellent (1) ............................ to choose from. If you cannot afford one of these, the (2) ............................ is very cheap and a good place to meet other young people. If you like to cook for yourself, there are many attractive (3) ............................ , some with their own swimming pool. If all you want is somewhere to sleep and eat breakfast, you could try a (4) ............................ . Finally, if you have a (5) ............................ , there are several very good campsites in the south.

## C Match the things you should do on the left with the reasons on the right. Write the letters in the box below.

Before you go on holiday abroad you should:

**1** buy some foreign currency

**2** buy a guidebook

**3** have vaccinations if you need them

**4** get a visa if you need it

**a** to find out more about the country you are going to

**b** to stop you from getting diseases

**c** so that you can get into the country you are going to

**d** so that you can buy things

| 1 .......... | 2 .......... | 3 .......... | 4 .......... |
|---|---|---|---|

# 25 Hotels

## A Match the words on the left with the definitions on the right. Write the letters in the box below.

| | |
|---|---|
| 1 room service | a a room in a hotel with two beds |
| 2 half board | b a person in a hotel who deals with guests when they arrive |
| 3 receptionist | c when you have food or drink brought to your room in a hotel |
| 4 full board | d having a bathroom attached |
| 5 reception | e when you pay only to have a room, your breakfast and dinner in a hotel |
| 6 double room | f an arrangement to have a room in a hotel |
| 7 single room | g make an arrangement to have a room in a hotel |
| 8 twin room | h when you pay to have a room and all your meals in a hotel |
| 9 book | i a room in a hotel with one bed for two people |
| 10 fully booked | j the place you go to in a hotel when you arrive |
| 11 ensuite | k when all the rooms in a hotel are being used |
| 12 reservation | l a room in a hotel with one bed for one person |

| | | | | | |
|---|---|---|---|---|---|
| 1 ........ | 2 ........ | 3 ........ | 4 ........ | 5 ........ | 6 ........ |
| 7 ........ | 8 ........ | 9 ........ | 10 ........ | 11 ........ | 12 ........ |

## B Complete the phone conversation with words from A.

Receptionist: Hello, The Wiseman Arms Hotel. How can I help you?

Customer: Hello, I'd like to make a (1) .............................. , please. I'd like to (2) .............................. a room for two for the night of 6th October.

Receptionist: I'm sorry, but we're (3) .............................. that night.

Customer: What about the night of 27th October?

Receptionist: Yes, that would be fine. Would you like a double room or a (4) ..............................?

Customer: A double room, please.

Receptionist: We have a double room with an (5) .............................. bathroom.

Customer: That would be fine. Thank you.

# 26 Travelling by plane

## A Complete the sentences with the words in the box.

| arrivals | baggage reclaim | check-in desk | customs |
|---|---|---|---|
| departure lounge | departures | gate | passport control |

1 You go to .................................. when you are going somewhere by plane.
2 You say that you have arrived for your flight at the .................................. .
3 You show your passport at .................................. when you are leaving or coming into a country.
4 You wait in the .................................. until it is time to get on your plane.
5 You get on or off a plane at the .................................. .
6 You go to .................................. to get back your bags after your flight.
7 Your bags are checked for illegal goods when you are going into a country at .................................. .
8 You meet someone who is arriving after a flight at .................................. .

## B Complete what the flight attendant is saying with the words in the box.

| aboard | boarding card | flight | hand luggage |
|---|---|---|---|
| landing | life jacket | overhead locker | take-off |

1 Good morning, sir. Can I see your .................................. , please? 65C – that's towards the back on your left. Have a pleasant .................................. .

2 On behalf of the captain and the crew, I would like to welcome you .................................. .

3 Please put all .................................. in the .................................. .

4 There is a .................................. under your seat for use in an emergency.

5 Please remain seated during .................................. and .................................. .

# 27 In the countryside

**A** **Look at the picture and complete the sentences with the words in the box.**

| bridge farm fields ~~footpath~~ forest lake lane |
|---|
| mountains river valley village waterfall |

Take the (1) ........*footpath*........ until you get to the (2) .............................. .
Walk across the (3) .............................. and then follow the
(4) .............................. . Go across the small (5) .............................. .
Turn right when you see the (6) .............................. . You will see a
(7) .............................. in front of you. Walk through it and you will come
to a small (8) .............................. . In the distance, you will be able to see
the (9) .............................. and the (10) .............................. between them.
Walk to the other side of the lake and then go down the
(11) .............................. , which will take you to the (12) .............................. .

# 28 The weather

**A Complete the sentences with the words in the boxes. Use the words in the left-hand box more than once.**

| east north<br>south west | forecast frost hail icy sunshine<br>mild showers thunder and lightning |
|---|---|

Here is the weather (1) .................................. . Today, it's going to be mostly fine with plenty of (2) .................................. in the (3) .................................. . By the afternoon though there will be (4) .................................. in the (5) .................................. .

Tomorrow morning there will be (6) .................................. conditions throughout the whole country, so do be careful on the roads. There may also be some (7) .................................. in the (8) .................................. .

Later in the week the weather will improve although there may be some overnight (9) .................................. in the (10) .................................. – don't forget to protect any plants you have in the garden.

At the weekend there will be heavy rain with some (11) .................................. .................................. in the (12) .................................. . It will stay (13) .................................. in the (14) .................................. with temperatures of 10°c.

# 29 Animals

## A Put the words in the box into the correct group.

bear butterfly crab deer fly fox frog kangaroo
octopus owl rat shark spider whale

| animals with wings | animals that live in water | other |
|---|---|---|
| .................. | .................. | .................. |
| .................. | .................. | .................. |
| .................. | .................. | .................. |
| | .................. | .................. |
| | .................. | .................. |
| | | .................. |

## B Label the animals with words from A.

1 .................. 2 .................. 3 .................. 4 ..................

5 .................. 6 .................. 7 ..................

## C Complete the sentences with the other words from A.

1 An .................. stays awake at night.
2 A .................. moves around by jumping. It lives in Australia.
3 A .................. has eight legs and doesn't live in water.
4 A .................. walks sideways.
5 An .................. has eight legs.
6 A .................. has very sharp teeth.
7 A .................. has a beautiful pattern on its wings.

# 30 Parts of a car

## A Label the picture with the words in the box.

| boot bumper engine headlight indicator seatbelt tyre wheel windscreen windscreen wipers wing mirror |
|---|

1 ..................................
2 ..................................
3 ..................................
4 ..................................
5 ..................................
6 ..................................
7 ..................................
8 ..................................
9 ..................................
10 ..................................
11 ..................................

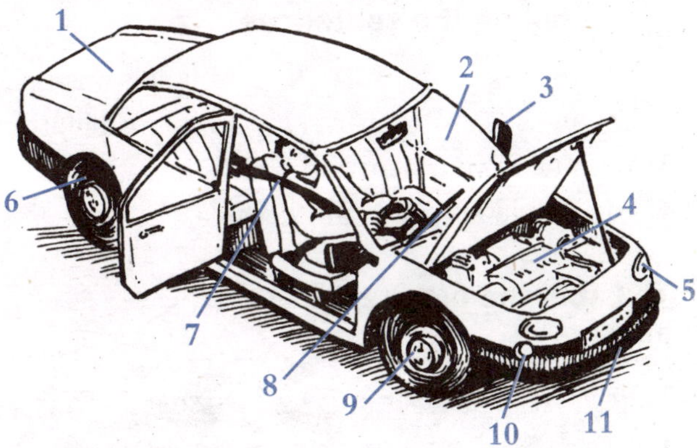


## B Complete the sentences with words from A. Remember to use the plural form if you need to.

1 If it's dark, remember to switch on the .................................. .

2 Before any journey, check that the .................................. have enough air in them.

3 It's a large car with room for lots of luggage in the .................................. .

4 Use the right .................................. to tell other drivers you are turning right.

5 Always fasten your .................................. before starting to drive.

6 If it's raining, turn on the .................................. .

# Test 3 (Units 21–30)

## A Complete the sentences with words for jobs.

1 I write for a local newspaper. I'm a ................................................ .

2 I work for the government. I'm a ................................................ .

3 I sell clothes in a department store. I'm a ................................................ .

4 I keep records of money for a company. I'm an ................................................ .

## B Complete the sentences.

1 You use a ................................................ to hold several pieces of paper together.

2 You use a ................................................ to do mathematical calculations.

3 You put all your pens and pencils in a ................................................ .

4 You should keep all your files in a ................................................ .

## C Label the picture.

1 ........................................

2 ........................................

3 ........................................

4 ........................................

5 ........................................

## D Complete the sentences.

1 If you've got a fax machine, you could send me a ................................................ .

2 If you've got a computer and a modem, you could send me an ........................................ .

3 If you've got a mobile phone, you could send me a ................................................ .

4 If you've got a pen, some writing paper and an envelope, you could send me a ........................................ .

# Test 3 (Units 21–30)

## E Complete the paragraphs with words for holidays, hotels and travelling by plane.

Last year I decided to go on a (1) ........................................ . I wanted to lie in the sun and swim in the sea for a change. I went on my own, so I called a hotel and (2) ........................................ a (3) ........................................ room. My (4) ........................................ was very early in the morning. While I was waiting in the (5) ........................................ after checking in, I bought myself a (6) ........................................ so that I could read about the area I was going to. I put it in my (7) ........................................ so that I could look at it on the plane. Actually, I finished reading it before (8) ........................................ – we had to wait two hours before we could leave because the pilot was ill.

## F Look at the picture and complete the sentences with words for the weather.

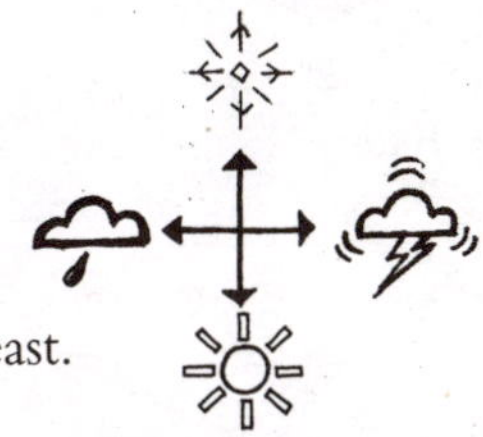

1 There will be ........................................ in the west.
2 There will be ........................................ in the north.
3 There will be ........................................ in the south.
4 There will be ........................................ in the east.

## G Put the letters in order. Then put the animals into the correct group.

| brac krash lewah lfy reutbylft wlo |
|---|

| animals that can fly | animals that can swim |
|---|---|
| ........................................ | ........................................ |
| ........................................ | ........................................ |
| ........................................ | ........................................ |

## H Complete the sentences about cars.

1 Can you see through the ........................................ ? It's really dirty.
2 Put that really big bag in the ........................................ .
3 Never drive without fastening your ........................................ .
4 What's wrong with the ........................................ ? The car's making a strange noise.

# 31 Everyday adjectives

## A Join the words with the opposite meanings.

| | |
|---|---|
| 1 smooth | light |
| 2 sharp | dry |
| 3 light | bent |
| 4 heavy | rough |
| 5 straight | dark |
| 6 wet | blunt |

## B Label the pictures with the words from A.

| | | | |
|---|---|---|---|
| 1  a .................... bag | 2  a .................... bag | 3  a .................... room | 4  a .................... room |
| 5  a .................... knife | 6 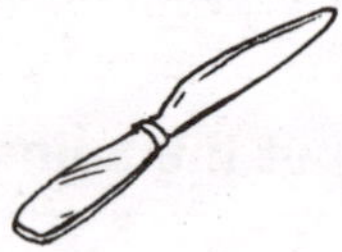 a .................... knife | 7  .................... hair | 8  .................... hair |
| 9 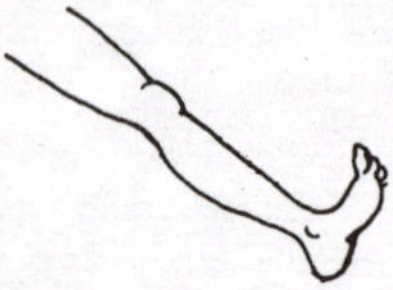 a .................... leg | 10 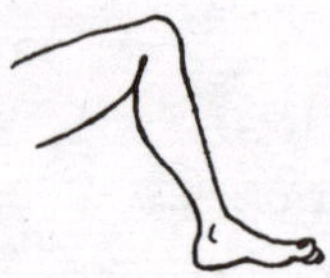 a .................... leg | 11 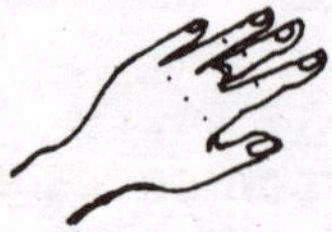 .................... skin | 12 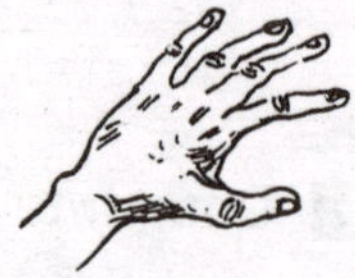 .................... skin |

# 32 Using your voice

## A Circle the correct verb and complete the sentence by writing it in the correct form.

| | |
|---|---|
| 1 'Shh, the baby's asleep,' she .................................... . | laugh / whisper |
| 2 Do you .................................... Japanese? | speak / stutter |
| 3 Can you two girls please stop .................................... ! | cheer / talk |
| 4 What did you .................................... at the concert? | shout / sing |
| 5 Don't .................................... . Mummy'll be back soon. | chat / cry |
| 6 'We're getting married,' he .................................... . | announce / tell |
| 7 'I want to go to bed,' he .................................... in a tired voice. | say / scream |

## B Complete the crossword with the other words from A.

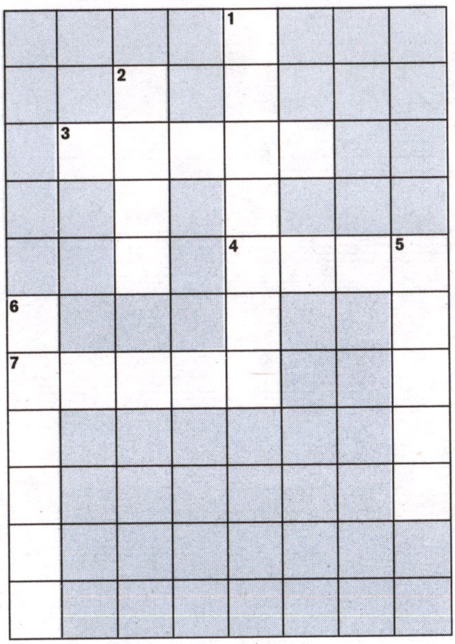


1 repeat the first part of a word several times because you have a speech problem
2 talk to someone in a friendly and informal way
3 say something very loudly
4 say something to someone, usually giving them information
5 make the sound of being happy or amused
6 cry or say something loudly, usually because you are afraid or angry
7 give a loud shout of encouragement

# 33 Using your hands

## A Label the pictures with the words in the box.

| clap knock pat pick pinch point scratch stroke tickle wave |
|---|

1 ..............................
2 ..............................
3 ..............................
4 ..............................
5 ..............................
6 ..............................
7 ..............................
8 ..............................
9 ..............................
10 ..............................

## B Use the expressions in the box and write sentences to describe the pictures in A.

| her arm the little boy the cat on the door his head the dog's head a flower ~~to his friend~~ to a word because they enjoyed the show |
|---|

1 *He's waving to his friend.*
2 ..............................
3 ..............................
4 ..............................
5 ..............................
6 ..............................
7 ..............................
8 ..............................
9 ..............................
10 ..............................

# 34 Do and make

**A** **Put the words in the box into the correct group.**

| ~~business~~ a cake exercise friends your homework the housework a mistake money a noise your teeth |
|---|

| do | make |
|---|---|
| business | ………… |
| ………… | ………… |
| ………… | ………… |
| ………… | ………… |
| ………… | ………… |

**B** **Match the words in the box with the pictures. Complete the phrases with *do* and *make*.**

| an appointment the bed a cup of tea the dishes an exam your hair lunch a phone call the shopping ~~a speech~~ |
|---|

1 make a speech
2 …………
3 …………
4 …………
5 …………
6 …………
7 …………
8 …………
9 …………
10 …………

# 35 Irregular past tenses

**A** **Put the letters in order to find the past tense of the verbs in the list.**

| roftog | dunof | tsol | guatht | melts | ~~tib~~ | webl |
|---|---|---|---|---|---|---|
| oder | tpu | petk | rewd | boker | hrtwe | werg |

| | | | |
|---|---|---|---|
| 1 bite | bit | 8 keep | ................ |
| 2 blow | ................ | 9 lose | ................ |
| 3 break | ................ | 10 put | ................ |
| 4 draw | ................ | 11 ride | ................ |
| 5 find | ................ | 12 smell | ................ |
| 6 forget | ................ | 13 teach | ................ |
| 7 grow | ................ | 14 throw | ................ |

**B** **Complete the sentences with the verbs in the past tense from A.**

1 No one had been in the house for years and it ................ horrible.
2 He ................ the ball to her.
3 I ................ my wallet while I was out shopping the other day.
4 We ................ our bikes all the way to the beach.
5 He ................ the flowers in some water.
6 He was going to stroke the dog, but it ................ him on the leg.
7 She ................ on her tea before drinking it.
8 We looked everywhere for the key, but we never ................ it.
9 I ................ to send him a birthday card.
10 I ................ the photos for a long time before throwing them out.
11 All the children ................ pictures of themselves.
12 Who ................ my glasses? Fixing them will be very expensive.
13 She ................ English in Japan for three years.
14 She ................ about 2cm last year.

# 36 Phrasal verbs with *off* and *up*

## A Complete the phrasal verbs with *off* or *up*.

1 I've tried to give .................... smoking, but it's very difficult.
2 Put the milk in the fridge, so it doesn't go .................... .
3 The plane took .................... 30 minutes late.
4 I was brought .................... by my grandparents.
5 My mum's always telling me .................... for putting my feet on the chairs.
6 I'm saving .................... to buy myself a DVD player.
7 When I grow .................... , I'd like to be a doctor.
8 Nobody likes him – he's always showing .................... .
9 You really should phone her. Why do you keep putting it .................... ?
10 If you don't hurry .................... , we're going to be late.

## B Label the pictures with phrasal verbs from A.

1 ....grow up....  2 ....................  3 ....................

4 ....................  5 ....................  6 ....................

## C Match the other phrasal verbs from A with the definitions.

1 look after and teach a child until they are old enough to look after themselves ....bring up....
2 something you say to someone when you want them to do something quickly ....................
3 stop doing something that you usually do ....................
4 become too old and bad to eat ....................

# 37 More phrasal verbs

**A** **Complete the sentences with the verbs in the box. Use each verb twice and remember to put the verb in the correct form.**

| fill get look run take |
|---|

1 Were you frightened? Why did you ......run...... away?
2 He had flu and it took him a long time to .................... over it.
3 If you want a credit card, you'll have to .................... in this form.
4 .................... out! There's a car coming.
5 Do you .................... on with your boyfriend's family?
6 They were .................... over by a bigger company last year.
7 Who .................... after the children when you're at work?
8 We've .................... out of milk – do you mind black coffee?
9 I went round the room .................... up everyone's glass.
10 In character, do you .................... after your mum or your dad?

**B** **Label the pictures with phrasal verbs from A.**

1 .................... 2 .................... 3 .................... 4 ....................

**C** **Match the other phrasal verbs from A with the definitions.**

1 take care of someone ....................
2 be similar to an older member of your family ....................
3 write information on an official document ....................
4 have a good relationship with someone ....................
5 feel better after being ill ....................
6 take control of something ....................

# 38 Sorry and thank you

## A Complete the sentences with the words in the box.

| apologise | matter | mention | mind | ~~OK~~ | problem |
|---|---|---|---|---|---|
| sorry | thank | thanks | welcome | worry | |

1 You'll have to wait another 15 minutes. — That's ..........OK.......... . I'm not in a hurry.

2 Thanks for telling me about this. — No .................................... . I thought you should know about it.

3 We're so late. We've missed the train now, haven't we? — Yes, but it doesn't .................................... . We can catch the next one.

4 It was really very kind of you to give me a lift home. — Oh, don't .................................... it. I was coming past your house anyway.

5 I upset him because I said I thought his hair looked terrible. — That wasn't very nice. I think you should .................................... .

6 I've done the dishes and tidied the living room for you. — Oh, .................................... you for doing all that. You really didn't have to.

7 I'm afraid we won't be able to come on Saturday night. — Oh well, never .................................... . We'll see you on Sunday anyway.

8 It's so untidy in here. — I'm .................................... . I haven't had time to tidy up yet.

9 Oops! I've spilt some of my drink. — Don't .................................... . It'll clean off easily.

10 Have another drink. — Oh, .................................... .

11 Thank you so much for the lovely flowers. — You're .................................... .

# 39 Giving directions

## A Complete the dialogue with the phrases in the box.

| car park  could you tell me the way to  go past  go straight on  junction  keep going  roundabout  take the first on the left  take the second exit  take the second on the right  traffic lights  turn left  turn left  turn right  turn right |
|---|

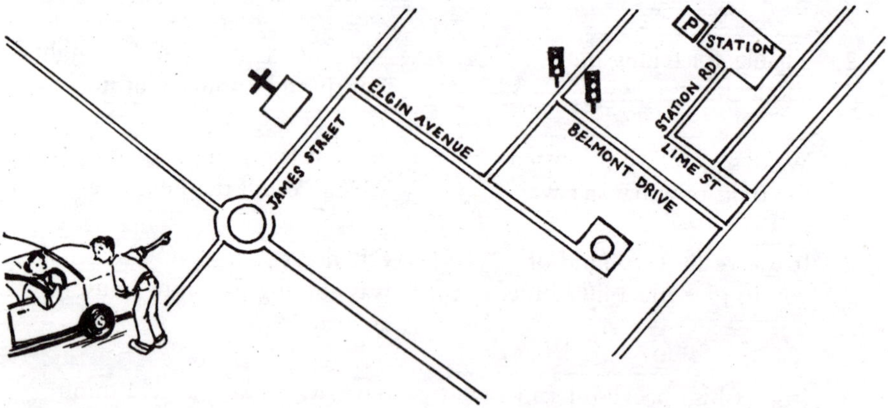


Driver: (1) .................................... the station, please?

Pedestrian: (2) .................................... until you come to the (3) .................................... . At the roundabout (4) .................................... into James Street. (5) .................................... the church on your left and (6) .................................... into Elgin Avenue. Then (7) .................................... and (8) .................................... as far as the (9) .................................... . Then (10) .................................... into Belmont Drive. At the next (11) .................................... – this should be a T- junction – (12) .................................... . Then (13) .................................... again into Lime Street and (14) .................................... . This is Station Road and the station is right at the end. You'll see the (15) .................................... right next to it.

# 40 On the phone

**A** **Complete the sentences with the words in the box. Remember to put the verbs in the correct form.**

| answer | calling | engaged | hang up | Hello | machine |
|---|---|---|---|---|---|
| message | mobile | pick | public | speak | wrong |

I was out shopping when I remembered I was supposed to call my friend about going out that evening. I looked everywhere for a (1) .................................. phone, but couldn't find one anywhere. Then I remembered I had my (2) .................................. phone in my bag. The first few times I called it was (3) .................................. . I thought she was probably talking to her boyfriend. They're always calling each other. The next time I tried there was no (4) .................................. , so I left a (5) .................................. on the answering (6) .................................. , telling her to call me. I waited and waited, but she didn't call, so I tried again. Finally someone (7) .................................. up the phone and said '(8) .................................. .'

'Could I (9) .................................. to Donna, please?' I asked.

'Who's (10) .................................. , please?' the person asked.

'It's Tina,' I said.

Then to my surprise, he just said, 'Sorry, I think you've got the (11) .................................. number.' And then he just (12) .................................. .

# Test 4 (Units 31–40)

## A Write the opposites of these adjectives.

1 bent ..............................

2 dark ..............................

3 smooth ..............................

4 dry ..............................

5 heavy ..............................

6 sharp ..............................

## B Complete the sentences with *do* or *make* or another verb that has an irregular past tense. Remember to put the verbs in the correct form.

I've had a terrible day. I got up at six o'clock, (1) .............................. the bed, had a shower, (2) .............................. my teeth and went downstairs. I (3) .............................. the dishes from yesterday and (4) .............................. myself a nice cup of tea. But then I dropped the milk jug and it (5) .............................. into pieces. I cleaned it up and decided to (6) .............................. the shopping. I (7) .............................. to take my wallet, so I had to walk all the way home again. It was twelve o'clock by this time, so I (8) .............................. lunch. After lunch I (9) .............................. a few phone calls and decided to go out again. Even before I got to the shops a big dog ran at me and (10) .............................. me on the leg. Now I'm at the hospital waiting to see a doctor.

## C The underlined words are in the wrong sentences. Write the correct word for each sentence.

1 If you are frightened, you clap. ..............................

2 If you are saying hello or goodbye to someone, you scream. ..............................

3 If you want to show someone where something is, you cry. ..............................

4 If you think someone's performance is very good, you whisper. ..............................

5 If you think something is funny, you wave. ..............................

6 If you don't want someone to hear what you are saying, you knock. ..............................

7 If you are sad, you laugh. ..............................

8 If you want to enter someone's room, you point. ..............................

# Test 4 (Units 31–40)

**D** **Write the correct words to complete the phrasal verbs.**

1 fill .................... this form fill .................... your glass
2 take .................... your father take .................... a company
3 get .................... your colleagues get .................... the flu

**E** **Join the sentences on the left with the replies on the right.**

| | | |
|---|---|---|
| 1 | Here, have a chocolate. | You're welcome. |
| 2 | Sorry, I can't go tonight. | Oh, sorry. |
| 3 | Thank you so much. | It doesn't matter. |
| 4 | You've spilt your drink on my coat. | Thank you. |

**F** **Write the directions for each picture.**

1 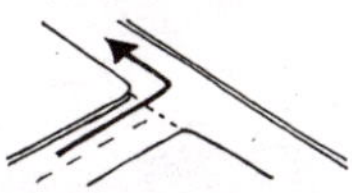

....................................................
....................................................

2 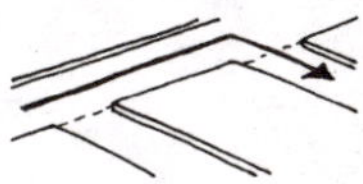

....................................................
....................................................

3 

....................................................
....................................................

4 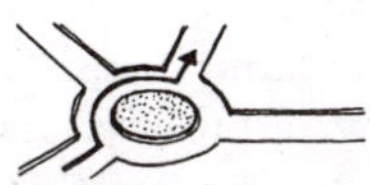

....................................................
....................................................

**G** **Complete the sentences.**

1 If you ring and I'm not in, .................................................... on the answering machine.
2 Who were you talking to? I rang, but it was .................................................... .
3 Please don't .................................................... . I need to talk to you.
4 I rang, but there was .................................................... . No one was in.
5 Is that 8893 1597? No? Oh sorry, I've got the .................................................... .

# Answer Key

## 1 The family

**A** **1** *son-in-law*
**2** step-father
**3** grandparents
**4** daughter-in-law
**5** step-son
**6** step-daughter
**7** mother-in-law
**8** brother-in-law
**9** step-mother
**10** great-grandmother
**11** great-grandfather
**12** father-in-law
**13** sister-in-law
**14** step-sister
**15** step-brother

## 2 People you know

**A** **family**
relative
**school**
classmate
**where you live**
neighbour
**love**
boyfriend
girlfriend
**work**
boss
colleague
**other**
*acquaintance*
close friend
friend of the family
mate

**B** **1** *mates*
**2** an acquaintance
**3** boss
**4** colleagues
**5** classmates
**6** neighbours
**7** relatives
**8** boyfriend
**9** friend of the family
**10** girlfriend
**11** a close friend

## 3 Clothes

**A** **beach holiday**
bikini
sandals
sunglasses
sunhat
swimming costume
trunks
**walking holiday**
fleece
walking boots
waterproof jacket

**B** **1** sandals
**2** bikini
**3** swimming costume
**4** walking boots
**5** sunhat
**6** trunks
**7** waterproof jacket
**8** fleece
**9** sunglasses

**C** **1** *slippers*
**2** dressing gown
**3** knickers
**4** nightie
**5** underpants
**6** bra
**7** pyjamas
**8** vest

## 4 Clothes and accessories

**A** **1** *lipstick*
**2** earrings
**3** comb
**4** wallet
**5** bracelet
**6** shoelaces
**7** ring
**8** belt
**9** purse
**10** necklace

## 5 Life

**A** **1** was born **2** moved house **3** grew up **4** started school **5** went to university **6** fell in love **7** got engaged **8** got married **9** had a baby **10** retired **11** got divorced **12** died

## 6 Describing character

**A**

| **bad qualities** | **good qualities** |
|---|---|
| impatient | generous |
| mean | lovely |
| rude | patient |
| selfish | polite |
| silly | sensible |

**B** **1** j **2** a **3** d **4** f **5** b **6** e **7** c **8** i **9** h **10** g

## 7 Describing appearance

**A** **1** cute **2** dark-skinned **3** elegant **4** fair-skinned **5** good-looking **6** overweight **7** plain **8** pretty **9** scruffy **10** slim **11** smart **12** trendy

**B** **1** good-looking **2** smart **3** overweight **4** fair-skinned **5** cute **6** plain **7** dark-skinned **8** trendy **9** scruffy **10** pretty **11** slim **12** elegant

## 8 How you feel

**A** **1** *cheerful* **2** relaxed **3** pleased **4** annoyed **5** proud **6** fed up

**B** **1** *miserable* **2** jealous **3** guilty **4** surprised **5** worried **6** embarrassed

## 9 Having a bad day

**A** **1** h **2** c **3** j **4** f **5** a **6** d **7** e **8** i **9** b **10** g

**B** **1** *overslept* **2** missed **3** was late **4** fell over **5** got lost **6** were stuck in a traffic jam **7** ran out of **8** broke down **9** spilt **10** had an argument

## 10 Accidents and injuries

**A** **1** *swollen; d* **2** burn; c **3** broken; b **4** cut; f **5** black; a **6** bruise; e

**B** **1** had an accident **2** unconscious **3** injured **4** bleeding **5** pain **6** treatment **7** stitches **8** hurt **9** bandage

## Test 1 (Units 1–10)

**A**
1. brother-in-law
2. colleague
3. neighbour
4. mother-in-law
5. step-mother
6. great-grandfather
7. boss
8. step-son

**B Gemma**
**appearance**
overweight
plain
scruffy
**clothes and accessories**
dressing gown
pyjamas
slippers
**Sarah**
**appearance**
pretty
slim
smart
**clothes and accessories**
bikini
bracelet
earrings
necklace
sandals
sunglasses
sunhat

**C**
1. be born
2. start school
3. fall in love
4. get engaged
5. get married
6. have a baby
7. retire
8. die

**D**
1. generous
2. selfish
3. silly
4. impatient
5. rude
6. sensible

**E**
1. miserable, had an argument
2. embarrassed, fell over
3. annoyed, spilt
4. guilty, had an accident
5. worried, is late
6. pleased, isn't in pain

**F**
1. stitches
2. burn
3. bandage
4. swollen
5. unconscious
6. bruise

## 11 Shops and shopping

**A**
1. supermarket
2. department store
3. chemist's
4. newsagent's
5. hairdresser's
6. trolley
7. clothes shop
8. butcher's
9. baker's
10. basket
11. gift shop
12. checkout

**B**
1. shop assistant
2. try on
3. fit
4. changing room
5. cost
6. till
7. pay
8. receipt

## 12 Houses and homes

**A**
1. *I live in a house.*
2. I live in a bungalow.
3. I live in a cottage.
4. I live in a flat.

**B**
1. detached
2. block of
3. semi-detached
4. terraced

**C**
1. ground floor
2. second floor
3. first floor
4. basement

## 13 Housework

**A**
1 duster
2 vacuum cleaner
3 washing machine
4 dustbin
5 washing line
6 pegs
7 dishwasher
8 iron
9 ironing board

**B**
**do the dishes**
dishwasher
**do the ironing**
iron
ironing board
**do the washing**
pegs
washing line
washing machine
**dust**
duster
**hoover**
vacuum cleaner
**put the rubbish out**
dustbin

## 14 In the kitchen

**A**
1 pan
2 corkscrew
3 tap
4 mug
5 tin opener
6 tea towel
7 frying pan
8 bottle opener
9 food processor
10 coffee maker
11 washing-up liquid
12 teapot

**B**
**for cleaning**
tap
tea towel
washing-up liquid
**for opening things**
bottle opener
corkscrew
tin opener
**for drinks**
coffee maker
mug
teapot
**for cooking**
food processor
frying pan
pan

## 15 Food

**A**
*bread rolls*
cereal
cucumber
eggs
frozen vegetables
melon
pineapple
tinned fruit

**B**
1 sausages
2 bacon
3 cheese
4 red pepper
5 aubergine
6 dried fruit

## 16 Health and fitness

**A**
1 *healthy*
2 fit
3 lose weight
4 be good for you
5 exercise
6 keep fit
7 be bad for you
8 unfit
9 healthy diet
10 put on weight
11 unhealthy

**B**
1 *fit*
2 healthy
3 lose weight
4 put on weight
5 bad for you
6 unhealthy
7 good for you
8 healthy diet
9 exercise
10 keep fit
11 unfit

## 17 Sport

**A**
1 pitch
2 court
3 track

**B**
1 match
2 player
3 score
4 goal
5 team
6 win
7 lose
8 game
9 scored
10 point
11 win
12 player
13 win
14 race

## 18 Music

**A** **types of music**
classical music
jazz
opera
pop music

**people**
band
choir
composer
conductor
orchestra
pop star
singer

**B**
1 I like jazz.
2 I like opera.
3 I like pop music.
4 I like classical music.

**C**
1 singer
2 conductor
3 orchestra
4 choir
5 composer
6 band
7 pop star

## 19 Shapes

**A**
1 *star*
2 circle
3 rectangle
4 squares
5 circle
6 hearts
7 oval
8 diamonds
9 rectangle
10 triangles
11 triangle
12 circles

**B**
1 square, square, rectangular, triangular
2 star-shaped, circular
3 heart-shaped
4 oval, triangular
5 diamond-shaped

## 20 Measurements

**A** **swimming pool**
1 length
2 width
3 depth

**man**
1 height
2 weight

**B**
1 long
2 heavy
3 wide
4 high
5 tall
6 deep
7 weigh

## Test 2 (Units 11–20)

**A**
1 newsagent's
2 chemist's
3 terraced
4 cottage

**B**
1 hoover
2 dishes
3 ironing
4 dust

**C**
1 tea towel
2 corkscrew
3 frying pan
4 bottle opener
5 teapot
6 tin opener

**D**
1 eggs
2 bacon
3 cheese
4 sausage

**E**
1 unfit
2 race
3 healthy
4 scored

**F**
1 jazz
2 orchestra
3 choir
4 composer

**G**

**H**
1 length
2 heavy
3 width
4 tall

## 21 Jobs

**A** **1** a cleaner
**2** a photographer
**3** an accountant
**4** a civil servant
**5** a computer programmer

**B** **1** *Eric*, Tim, Michelle
**2** Janice, Lena

**C** **1** journalist
**2** model
**3** au pair
**4** shop assistant

## 22 In the office

**A** **1** filing cabinet
**2** file
**3** desk tidy
**4** Post-it™ note
**5** notepad
**6** diary
**7** ring binder
**8** calculator
**9** stapler
**10** paper clip
**11** hole punch
**12** in-tray/out-tray

**B** **1** paper clip
**2** stapler
**3** desk tidy
**4** Post-it™ note
**5** notepad
**6** diary

## 23 Writing to people

**A** **1** a memo
**2** a letter
**3** a postcard
**4** an email
**5** a note
**6** a fax
**7** a text message

**B** **1** writing paper
**2** postcode
**3** address
**4** stamp
**5** envelope

## 24 Holidays

**A** **1** camping holiday
**2** beach holiday
**3** walking holiday
**4** skiing holiday
**5** cruise

**B** **1** hotels
**2** youth hostel
**3** villas
**4** bed and breakfast
**5** tent

**C** **1** d
**2** a
**3** b
**4** c

## 25 Hotels

**A** **1** c
**2** e
**3** b
**4** h
**5** j
**6** i
**7** l
**8** a
**9** g
**10** k
**11** d
**12** f

**B** **1** reservation
**2** book
**3** fully booked
**4** twin room
**5** ensuite

## 26 Travelling by plane

**A** **1** departures
**2** check-in desk
**3** passport control
**4** departure lounge
**5** gate
**6** baggage reclaim
**7** customs
**8** arrivals

**B** **1** boarding card, flight
**2** aboard
**3** hand luggage, overhead locker
**4** life jacket
**5** take-off, landing

## 27 In the countryside

**A** **1** *footpath* **2** farm **3** fields **4** river **5** bridge **6** waterfall **7** forest **8** lake **9** mountains **10** valley **11** lane **12** village

## 28 The weather

**A** **1** forecast **2** sunshine **3** south **4** showers **5** west **6** icy **7** hail **8** east **9** frost **10** east **11** thunder and lightning **12** north **13** mild **14** south

## 29 Animals

**A** **animals with wings**
butterfly
fly
owl

**animals that live in water**
crab
frog
octopus
shark
whale

**other**
bear
deer
fox
kangaroo
rat
spider

**B** **1** bear **2** rat **3** frog **4** whale **5** fly **6** deer **7** fox

**C** **1** owl **2** kangaroo **3** spider **4** crab **5** octopus **6** shark **7** butterfly

## 30 Parts of a car

**A** **1** boot **2** windscreen **3** wing mirror **4** engine **5** headlight **6** tyre **7** seatbelt **8** windscreen wipers **9** wheel **10** indicator **11** bumper

**B** **1** headlights **2** tyres **3** boot **4** indicator **5** seatbelt **6** windscreen wipers

## Test 3 (Units 21–30)

**A** 1 journalist
2 civil servant
3 shop assistant
4 accountant

**B** 1 paper clip
2 calculator
3 desk tidy
4 filing cabinet

**C** 1 mountains
2 lake
3 river
4 waterfall
5 bridge

**D** 1 fax
2 email
3 text message
4 letter

**E** 1 beach holiday
2 booked
3 single
4 flight
5 departure lounge
6 guidebook
7 hand luggage
8 take-off

**F** 1 showers
2 frost
3 sunshine
4 thunder and lightning

**G** **animals that can fly**
fly
butterfly
owl
**animals that can swim**
crab
shark
whale

**H** 1 windscreen
2 boot
3 seatbelt
4 engine

## 31 Everyday adjectives

**A** 1 *rough*
2 blunt
3 dark
4 light
5 bent
6 dry

**B** 1 heavy
2 light
3 dark
4 light
5 sharp
6 blunt
7 dry
8 wet
9 straight
10 bent
11 smooth
12 rough

## 32 Using your voice

**A** 1 whispered
2 speak
3 talking
4 sing
5 cry
6 announced
7 said

**B** 1 stutter
2 chat
3 shout
4 tell
5 laugh
6 scream
7 cheer

## 33 Using your hands

**A** 1 wave
2 clap
3 pick
4 tickle
5 point
6 stroke
7 pat
8 pinch
9 knock
10 scratch

**B** 1 *He's waving to his friend.*
2 They're clapping because they enjoyed the show.
3 She's picking a flower.
4 She's tickling the little boy.
5 He's pointing to a word.
6 She's stroking the cat.
7 They're patting the dog's head.
8 He's pinching her arm.
9 She's knocking on the door.
10 He's scratching his head.

## 34 *Do* and *make*

**A**

| **do** | **make** |
|---|---|
| *business* | a cake |
| exercise | friends |
| your homework | a mistake |
| the housework | money |
| your teeth | a noise |

**B** **1** *make a speech* **2** make the bed **3** do the shopping **4** make a phone call **5** do an exam **6** make a cup of tea **7** make an appointment **8** do your hair **9** do the dishes **10** make lunch

## 35 Irregular past tenses

**A** **1** *bit* **2** blew **3** broke **4** drew **5** found **6** forgot **7** grew **8** kept **9** lost **10** put **11** rode **12** smelt **13** taught **14** threw

**B** **1** smelt **2** threw **3** lost **4** rode **5** put **6** bit **7** blew **8** found **9** forgot **10** kept **11** drew **12** broke **13** taught **14** grew

## 36 Phrasal verbs with *off* and *up*

**A** **1** up **2** off **3** off **4** up **5** off **6** up **7** up **8** off **9** off **10** up

**B** **1** *grow up* **2** take off **3** put off **4** save up **5** tell off **6** show off

**C** **1** *bring up* **2** hurry up **3** give up **4** go off

## 37 More phrasal verbs

**A** **1** *run* **2** get **3** fill **4** Look **5** get **6** taken **7** looks **8** run **9** filling **10** take

**B** **1** fill up **2** run out **3** run away **4** look out

**C** **1** look after **2** take after **3** fill in **4** get on with **5** get over **6** take over

## 38 Sorry and thank you

**A** **1** *OK* **2** problem **3** matter **4** mention **5** apologise **6** thank **7** mind **8** sorry **9** worry **10** thanks **11** welcome

## 39 Giving directions

**A** **1** Could you tell me the way to
**2** Go straight on
**3** roundabout
**4** take the second exit
**5** Go past
**6** turn right
**7** take the first on the left
**8** keep going
**9** traffic lights
**10** turn right
**11** junction
**12** turn left
**13** turn left
**14** take the second on the right
**15** car park

## 40 On the phone

**A** **1** public
**2** mobile
**3** engaged
**4** answer
**5** message
**6** machine
**7** picked
**8** Hello
**9** speak
**10** calling
**11** wrong
**12** hung up

## Test 4 (Units 31–40)

**A** **1** straight
**2** light
**3** rough
**4** wet
**5** light
**6** blunt

**B** **1** made
**2** did
**3** did
**4** made
**5** broke
**6** do
**7** forgot
**8** made
**9** made
**10** bit

**C** **1** scream
**2** wave
**3** point
**4** clap
**5** laugh
**6** whisper
**7** cry
**8** knock

**D** **1** in, up
**2** after, over
**3** on with, over

**E** **1** Thank you.
**2** It doesn't matter.
**3** You're welcome.
**4** Oh, sorry.

**F** **1** turn left
**2** take the second on the right
**3** go past
**4** take the second exit

**G** **1** leave a message
**2** engaged
**3** hang up
**4** no answer
**5** wrong number

# Word List

The words in this list are British English. Sometimes we give you an important American English word which means the same.

## 1 The family

brother-in-law /ˈbrʌðərɪnlɔː/
daughter-in-law /ˈdɔːtərɪnlɔː/
father-in-law /ˈfɑːðərɪnlɔː/
grandparents /ˈɡrænˌpeərənts/
great-grandfather /ˌɡreɪtˈɡrænˌfɑːðə/
great-grandmother /ˌɡreɪtˈɡrænˌmʌðə/
mother-in-law /ˈmʌðərɪnlɔː/
sister-in-law /ˈsɪstərɪnlɔː/
son-in-law /ˈsʌnɪnlɔː/
step-brother /ˈstepbrʌðə/
step-daughter /ˈstepdɔːtə/
step-father /ˈstepfɑːðə/
step-mother /ˈstepmʌðə/
step-sister /ˈstepsɪstə/
step-son /ˈstepsʌn/

## 2 People you know

acquaintance /əˈkweɪntəns/
boss /bɒs/
boyfriend /ˈbɔɪfrend/
classmate /ˈklɑːsmeɪt/
close friend /ˌkləʊs ˈfrend/
colleague /ˈkɒliːɡ/
friend of the family /ˌfrend əv ðə ˈfæməli/
girlfriend /ˈɡɜːlfrend/
mate /meɪt/ (informal)
neighbour /ˈneɪbə/
relative /ˈrelətɪv/

## 3 Clothes

bikini /bɪ'kiːni/
bra /brɑː/
dressing gown /'dresɪŋ gaʊn/ (US = robe)
fleece /fliːs/
knickers /'nɪkəz/ (Use with a plural verb, e.g. My knickers *are* white. Or a pair of knickers. US = panties)
nightie /'naɪti/
pyjamas /pɪ'dʒɑːməz/ (US = pajamas)
sandals /'sændəlz/
slippers /'slɪpəz/
sunglasses /'sʌnˌglɑːsɪz/
sunhat /'sʌn hæt/
swimming costume /'swɪmɪŋ ˌkɒstjuːm/ (US = bathing suit)
trunks /trʌŋks/ (Use with a plural verb, e.g. My trunks *are* green.)
underpants /'ʌndəpænts/ (Use with a plural verb, e.g. My underpants *are* white. Or a pair of underpants)
vest /vest/ (US = undershirt)
walking boots /'wɔːkɪŋ buːts/
waterproof jacket /ˌwɔːtəpruːf 'dʒækɪt/

## 4 Clothes and accessories

belt /belt/
bracelet /'breɪslət/
comb /kəʊm/
earrings /'ɪərɪŋz/
lipstick /'lɪpstɪk/
necklace /'nekləs/
purse /pɜːs/ (in US English this word means handbag)
ring /rɪŋ/
shoelaces /'ʃuːleɪsɪz/
wallet /'wɒlɪt/

## 5 Life

be born /biː 'bɔːn/ (*past tense* was/were; *past participle* been)
die /daɪ/
fall in love /ˌfɔːl ɪn 'lʌv/ (*past tense* fell; *past participle* fallen)
get divorced /ˌget dɪ'vɔːst/ (*past tense* & *past participle* got)

get engaged /ˌget ɪnˈgeɪdʒd/ (*past tense* & *past participle* got)
get married /ˌget ˈmærid/ (*past tense* & *past participle* got)
go to university /ˌgəʊ tə ˌjuːnɪˈvɜːsəti/ (*past tense* went; *past participle* gone)
grow up /ˌgrəʊ ˈʌp/ (*past tense* grew; *past participle* grown)
have a baby /ˌhæv ə ˈbeɪbi/ (*past tense* & *past participle* had)
move house /ˌmuːv ˈhaʊs/
start school /ˌstɑːt ˈskuːl/
retire /rɪˈtaɪə/

## 6 Describing character

generous /ˈdʒenərəs/
impatient /ɪmˈpeɪʃənt/
lovely /ˈlʌvli/
mean /miːn/
patient /ˈpeɪʃənt/
polite /pəˈlaɪt/
rude /ruːd/
selfish /ˈselfɪʃ/
sensible /ˈsensɪbl/
silly /ˈsɪli/

## 7 Describing appearance

cute /kjuːt/ (usually used about a child or baby. In US English also used about men and women)
dark-skinned /ˌdɑːkˈskɪnd/
elegant /ˈelɪgənt/ (used about a woman)
fair-skinned /ˌfeəˈskɪnd/
good-looking /ˌgʊdˈlʊkɪŋ/
overweight /ˌəʊvəˈweɪt/
plain /pleɪn/ (polite for *ugly*, usually used about a woman)
pretty /ˈprɪti/ (used about a woman)
scruffy /ˈskrʌfi/
slim /slɪm/ (an approving word)
smart /smɑːt/
trendy /ˈtrendi/ (an informal word)

## 8 How you feel

annoyed /ə'nɔɪd/
cheerful /'tʃɪəfəl/
embarrassed /ɪm'bærəst/
fed up /ˌfed 'ʌp/ (informal)
guilty /'gɪlti/
jealous /'dʒeləs/
miserable /'mɪzrəbl/
pleased /pliːzd/
proud /praʊd/
relaxed /rɪ'lækst/
surprised /sə'praɪzd/
worried /'wʌrid/

## 9 Having a bad day

be late /biː 'leɪt/ (*past tense* was/were; *past participle* been)
be stuck in a traffic jam /biː ˌstʌk ɪn ə 'træfɪk ˌdʒæm/
break down /ˌbreɪk 'daʊn/ (*past tense* broke; *past participle* broken)
fall over /ˌfɔːl 'əʊvə/ (*past tense* fell; *past participle* fallen)
get lost /ˌget 'lɒst/ (*past tense* & *past participle* got)
have an argument /ˌhæv ən 'ɑːgjəmənt/ (*past tense* & *past participle* had)
miss /mɪs/
oversleep /ˌəʊvə'sliːp/ (*past tense* & *past participle* overslept)
run out of /ˌrʌn 'aʊt əv/ (*past tense* ran; *past participle* run)
spill /spɪl/ (*past tense & past participle* spilled *UK also* spilt)

## 10 Accidents and injuries

bandage /'bændɪdʒ/
be in pain /biː ɪn 'peɪn/
black eye /ˌblæk 'aɪ/
bleed /bliːd/ (*past tense & past participle* bled)
broken /'brəʊkən/
bruise /bruːz/
burn /bɜːn/
cut /kʌt/
have an accident /hæv ən 'æksɪdənt/
hurt /hɜːt/ (*past tense & past participle* hurt)
injured /'ɪndʒəd/

stitches /ˈstɪtʃɪz/
swollen /ˈswəʊlən/
treatment /ˈtriːtmənt/
unconscious /ʌnˈkɒnʃəs/

## 11 Shops and shopping

baker's /ˈbeɪkəz/
basket /ˈbɑːskɪt/
butcher's /ˈbʊtʃəz/
changing room /ˈtʃeɪndʒɪŋ ˌruːm/
checkout /ˈtʃekaʊt/
chemist's /ˈkemɪsts/
clothes shop /ˈkləʊðz ʃɒp/
cost /kɒst/ (*past tense & past participle* cost)
department store /dɪˈpɑːtmənt ˌstɔː/
fit /fɪt/
gift shop /ˈgɪft ʃɒp/
hairdresser's /ˈheədresəz/
newsagent's /ˈnjuːzˌeɪdʒənts/
pay by cheque / credit card /ˌpeɪ ˈbaɪ tʃek / ˈkredɪt ˌkɑːd/
receipt /rɪˈsiːt/
shop assistant /ˈʃɒp əsɪstənt/
supermarket /ˈsuːpəˌmɑːkɪt/
till /tɪl/
trolley /ˈtrɒli/
try on /ˌtraɪ ˈɒn/

## 12 Houses and homes

basement /ˈbeɪsmənt/
block of flats /ˈblɒk əv flæts/
bungalow /ˈbʌŋgələʊ/
cottage /ˈkɒtɪdʒ/
detached /dɪˈtætʃt/
first floor /ˌfɜːst ˈflɔː/ (in US English this means ground floor)
flat /flæt/
ground floor /ˌgraʊnd ˈflɔː/
house /haʊs/
second floor /ˌsekənd ˈflɔː/ (in US English this means first floor)
semi-detached /ˌsemɪdɪˈtætʃt/
terraced /ˈterɪst/

## 13 Housework

dishwasher /ˈdɪʃˌwɒʃə/
do the dishes /ˌduː ðə ˈdɪʃɪz/
do the ironing /ˌduː ðɪ ˈaɪənɪŋ/
do the washing /ˌduː ðə ˈwɒʃɪŋ/
dust /dʌst/
dustbin /ˈdʌsbɪn/
duster /ˈdʌstə/
hoover /ˈhuːvə/
iron /ˈaɪən/
ironing board /ˈaɪənɪŋ ˌbɔːd/
pegs /pegz/
put the rubbish out /ˌpʊt ðə ˈrʌbɪʃ aʊt/
vacuum cleaner /ˈvækjuːm ˌkliːnə/
washing line /ˈwɒʃɪŋ ˌlaɪn/
washing machine /ˈwɒʃɪŋ məˌʃiːn/

## 14 In the kitchen

bottle opener /ˈbɒtl ˌəʊpənə/
coffee maker /ˈkɒfi meɪkə/
corkscrew /ˈkɔːkskruː/
food processor /ˈfuːd prəʊsesə/
frying pan /ˈfraɪɪŋ pæn/
mug /mʌg/
pan /pæn/
tap /tæp/
teapot /ˈtiːpɒt/
tea towel /ˈtiː ˌtaʊəl/
tin opener /ˈtɪn əʊpənə/
washing-up liquid /ˌwɒʃɪŋˈʌp ˌlɪkwɪd/

## 15 Food

aubergine /ˈəʊbəʒiːn/ (US = eggplant)
bacon /ˈbeɪkən/
bread rolls /ˌbred ˈrəʊlz/
cereal /ˈsɪəriəl/
cheese /tʃiːz/
cucumber /ˈkjuːkʌmbə/

dried fruit /ˌdraɪd 'fruːt/
eggs /egz/
frozen vegetables /ˌfrəʊzən 'vedʒtəblz/
melon /'melən/
red pepper /ˌred pepə/
pineapple /'paɪnæpl/
sausages /'sɒsɪdʒɪz/
tinned fruit /ˌtɪnd 'fruːt/

## 16 Health and fitness

be bad for you /biː 'bæd fə juː/
be good for you /biː 'gʊd fə juː/
exercise /'eksəsaɪz/
fit /fɪt/
healthy /'helθi/
healthy diet /ˌhelθi 'daɪət/
keep fit /ˌkiːp fɪt/
lose weight /ˌluːz 'weɪt/
put on weight /ˌpʊt ɒn 'weɪt/
unfit /ʌn'fɪt/
unhealthy /ʌn'helθi/

## 17 Sport

court /kɔːt/
game /geɪm/
goal /gəʊl/
lose /luːz/ (*past tense & past participle* lost)
match /mætʃ/
pitch /pɪtʃ/
player /pleɪə/
point /pɔɪnt/
race /reɪs/
score /skɔː/
team /tiːm/
track /træk/
win /wɪn/ (*past tense & past participle* won)

## 18 Music

band /bænd/
choir /kwaɪə/
classical music /ˌklæsɪkəl 'mjuːzɪk/
composer /kəm'pəʊzə/
conductor /kən'dʌktə/
jazz /dʒæz/
opera /'ɒpərə/
orchestra /'ɔːkɪstrə/
pop music /'pɒp ˌmjuːzɪk/
pop star /'pɒp ˌstɑː/
singer /'sɪŋə/

## 19 Shapes

circle /'sɜːkl/
circular /'sɜːkjələ/
diamond /'daɪəmənd/
diamond-shaped /'daɪəmәndʃeɪpt/
heart /hɑːt/
heart-shaped /'hɑːtʃeɪpt/
oval /əʊvəl/ (noun and adjective)
rectangle /'rektæŋgl/
rectangular /rek'tæŋgjələ/
square /skweə/ (noun and adjective)
star /stɑː/
star-shaped /'stɑːʃeɪpt/
triangle /'traɪæŋgl/
triangular /traɪ'æŋgjələ/

## 20 Measurements

deep /diːp/
depth /depθ/
heavy /'hevi/
height /haɪt/
high /haɪ/
length /leŋθ/
long /lɒŋ/

tall /tɔːl/ (how tall are you?)
weigh /weɪ/ (how much do you weigh?)
weight /weɪt/
wide /waɪd/
width /wɪtθ/

## 21 Jobs

accountant /əˈkaʊntənt/
au pair /ˌəʊˈpeə/
civil servant /ˌsɪvəl ˈsɜːvənt/
cleaner /ˈkliːnə/
computer programmer /kəmpjuːtə ˈprəʊgræmə/
full-time /ˌfʊlˈtaɪm/
journalist /ˈdʒɜːnəlɪst/
model /ˈmɒdəl/
part-time /ˌpɑːtˈtaɪm/
photographer /fəˈtɒgrəfə/
shop assistant /ˈʃɒp əsɪstənt/

## 22 In the office

calculator /ˈkælkjəleɪtə/
desk tidy /ˈdesk taɪdi/
diary /ˈdaɪəri/
file /faɪl/
filing cabinet /ˈfaɪlɪŋ ˌkæbɪnət/
hole punch /ˈhəʊl ˌpʌnʃ/
in-tray/out-tray /ˈɪntreɪ / ˈaʊttreɪ/
notepad /ˈnəʊtpæd/
paper clip /ˈpeɪpə klɪp/
Post-it™ note /ˈpəʊstɪt ˌnəʊt/
ring binder /ˈrɪŋ baɪndə/
stapler /ˈsteɪplə/

## 23 Writing to people

address /ə'dres/
email /'iːmeɪl/
envelope /'envələʊp/
fax /fæks/
letter /'letə/
memo /'meməʊ/
note /nəʊt/
postcard /'pəʊskɑːd/
postcode /'pəʊskəʊd/
stamp /stæmp/
text message /'tekst ˌmesɪdʒ/
writing paper /'raɪtɪŋ ˌpeɪpə/

## 24 Holidays

beach holiday /'biːtʃ ˌhɒlədeɪ/
bed and breakfast /bed ən 'brekfəst/
camping holiday /'kæmpɪŋ ˌhɒlədeɪ/
cruise /kruːz/
foreign currency /ˌfɒrɪn 'kʌrənsi/
guidebook /'gaɪdbʊk/
hotel /həʊ'tel/
skiing holiday /'skiːɪŋ ˌhɒlədeɪ/
tent /tent/
vaccination /ˌvæksɪ'neɪʃən/
villa /'vɪlə/
visa /'viːzə/
walking holiday /'wɔːkɪŋ ˌhɒlədeɪ/
youth hostel /'juːθ ˌhɒstəl/

## 25 Hotels

book /bʊk/
double room /ˌdʌbl 'ruːm/
ensuite /ˌɒn 'swiːt/
full board /ˌfʊl 'bɔːd/
fully booked /ˌfʊli 'bʊkt/
half board /ˌhɑːf 'bɔːd/
reception /rɪ'sepʃən/

receptionist /rɪˈsepʃənɪst/
reservation /ˌrezəˈveɪʃən/
room service /ˈruːm ˌsɜːvɪs/
single room /ˌsɪŋgl ˈruːm/
twin room /ˈtwɪn ˌruːm/

## 26 Travelling by plane

aboard /əˈbɔːd/
arrivals /əˈraɪvəlz/
baggage reclaim /ˈbægɪdʒ ˌrɪkleɪm/
boarding card /ˈbɔːdɪŋ ˌkɑːd/
check-in desk /ˈtʃekɪn ˌdesk/
customs /ˈkʌstəmz/
departure lounge /dɪˈpɑːtʃə ˌlaʊndʒ/
departures /dɪˈpɑːtʃəz/
flight /flaɪt/
gate /geɪt/
hand luggage /ˈhænd ˌlʌgɪdʒ/
landing /ˈlændɪŋ/
life jacket /ˈlaɪf ˌdʒækɪt/
overhead locker /ˌəʊvəhed ˈlɒkə/
passport control /ˈpɑːspɔːt ˌkəntrəʊl/
take-off /ˈteɪkɒf/

## 27 In the countryside

bridge /brɪdʒ/
farm /fɑːm/
fields /ˈfiːldz/
footpath /ˈfʊtpɑːθ/
forest /ˈfɒrɪst/
lake /leɪk/
lane /leɪn/
mountains /ˈmaʊntɪnz/
river /ˈrɪvə/
valley /ˈvæli/
village /ˈvɪlɪdʒ/
waterfall /ˈwɔːtəfɔːl/

## 28 The weather

east /iːst/
forecast /'fɔːkɑːst/
frost /frɒst/
hail /heɪl/
icy /'aɪsi/
lightning /'laɪtnɪŋ/
mild /maɪld/
north /nɔːθ/
showers /ʃaʊəz/
south /saʊθ/
sunshine /'sʌnʃaɪn/
thunder /'θʌndə/
west /west/

## 29 Animals

bear /beə/
butterfly /'bʌtəflaɪ/
crab /kræb/
deer /dɪə/ (plural = deer)
fly /flaɪ/
fox /fɒks/
frog /frɒg/
kangaroo /ˌkæŋgər'uː/
octopus /'ɒktəpəs/
owl /aʊl/
rat /ræt/
shark /ʃɑːk/
spider /'spaɪdə/
whale /weɪl/

## 30 Parts of a car

boot /buːt/ (US = trunk)
bumper /'bʌmpə/
engine /'endʒɪn/
headlight /'hedlaɪt/
indicator /'ɪndɪkeɪtə/
seatbelt /'siːtˌbelt/

tyre /taɪə/
wheel /wiːl/
windscreen /ˈwɪnskriːn/
windscreen wipers /ˈwɪnskriːn ˌwaɪpəz/
wing mirror /ˈwɪŋ ˌmɪrə/

## 31 Everyday adjectives

bent /bent/
blunt /blʌnt/
dark /dɑːk/
dry /draɪ/
heavy /ˈhevi/
light /laɪt/
rough /rʌf/
sharp /ʃɑːp/
smooth /smuːð/
straight /streɪt/
wet /wet/

## 32 Using your voice

announce /əˈnaʊns/
chat /tʃæt/
cheer /tʃɪə/
cry /kraɪ/
laugh /lɑːf/
say /seɪ/ (*past tense & past participle* said)
scream /skriːm/
shout /ʃaʊt/
sing /sɪŋ/ (*past tense* sang; *past participle* sung)
speak /spiːk/ (*past tense* spoke; *past participle* spoken)
stutter /ˈstʌtə/
talk /tɔːk/
tell /tel/ (*past tense & past participle* told)
whisper /ˈwɪspə/

## 33 Using your hands

clap /klæp/
knock /nɒk/
pat /pæt/
pick /pɪk/
pinch /pɪnʃ/
point /pɔɪnt/
scratch /skrætʃ/
stroke /strəʊk/
tickle /'tɪkl/
wave /weɪv/

## 34 *Do* and *make*

do business /ˌduː 'bɪznɪs/
do the dishes /ˌduː ðə 'dɪʃɪz/
do an exam /ˌduː ən ɪg'zæm/
do exercise /ˌduː 'eksəsaɪz/
do your hair /ˌduː jə heə/
do your homework /ˌduː jə 'həʊmwɜːk/
do the housework /ˌduː ðə 'haʊswɜːk/
do the shopping /ˌduː ðə 'ʃɒpɪŋ/
do your teeth /ˌduː jə 'tiːθ/
make an appointment /ˌmeɪk ən ə'pɔɪntmənt/
make the bed /ˌmeɪk ðə bed/
make a cake /ˌmeɪk ə 'keɪk/
make a cup of tea /ˌmeɪk ə ˌkʌp əv 'tiː/
make friends /ˌmeɪk 'frendz/
make lunch /ˌmeɪk 'lʌnʃ/
make a mistake /ˌmeɪk ə mɪs'teɪk/
make money /ˌmeɪk 'mʌni/
make a noise /ˌmeɪk ə 'nɔɪz/
make a phone call /ˌmeɪk ə 'fəʊn kɔːl/
make a speech /ˌmeɪk ə 'spiːtʃ/

## 35 Irregular past tenses

bite /baɪt/ (*past tense* bit; *past participle* bitten)
blow /bləʊ/ (*past tense* blew; *past participle* blown)
break /breɪk/ (*past tense* broke; *past participle* broken)

draw /drɔː/ (*past tense* drew; *past participle* drawn)
find /faɪnd/ (*past tense* & *past participle* found)
forget /fə'get/ (*past tense* forgot; *past participle* forgotten)
grow /grəʊ/ (*past tense* grew; *past participle* grown)
keep /kiːp/ (*past tense* & *past participle* kept)
lose /luːz/ (*past tense* & *past participle* lost)
put /pʊt/ (*past tense* & *past participle* put)
ride /raɪd/ (*past tense* rode; *past participle* ridden)
smell /smel/ (*past tense* & *past participle* smelled *UK also* smelt)
teach /tiːtʃ/ (*past tense* & *past participle* taught)
throw /θrəʊ/ (*past tense* threw; *past participle* thrown)

## 36 Phrasal verbs with *off* and *up*

bring up /ˌbrɪŋ 'ʌp/ (*past tense & past participle* brought)
give up /ˌgɪv 'ʌp/ (*past tense* gave; *past participle* given)
go off /ˌgəʊ 'ɒf/ (*past tense* went; *past participle* gone)
grow up /ˌgrəʊ 'ʌp/ (*past tense* grew; *past participle* grown)
hurry up /ˌhʌri 'ʌp/
put off /ˌpʊt 'ɒf/ (*past tense & past participle* put)
save up /ˌseɪv 'ʌp/
show off /ˌʃəʊ 'ɒf/ (*past tense* showed; *past participle* shown)
take off /ˌteɪk 'ɒf/ (*past tense* took; *past participle* taken)
tell off /ˌtel 'ɒf/ (*past tense & past participle* told)

## 37 More phrasal verbs

fill in /ˌfɪl 'ɪn/
fill up /ˌfɪl 'ʌp/
get on with /ˌget 'ɒn wɪð/ (*past tense* got; *past participle* got *US also* gotten)
get over /ˌget 'əʊvə/ (*past tense* got; *past participle* got *US also* gotten)
look after /ˌlʊk 'ɑːftə/
look out! /ˌlʊk 'aʊt/
run away /ˌrʌn 'əweɪ/ (*past tense* ran; *past participle* run)
run out of /ˌrʌn 'aʊt əv/ (*past tense* ran; *past participle* run)
take after /ˌteɪk 'ɑːftə/ (*past tense* took; *past participle* taken)
take over /ˌteɪk 'əʊvə/ (*past tense* took; *past participle* taken)

## 38 Sorry and thank you

apologise /ə'pɒlədʒaɪz/
don't mention it /ˌdəʊnt 'menʃən ɪt/
don't worry /ˌdəʊnt 'wʌri/
it doesn't matter /ɪt ˌdʌzənt 'mætə/
never mind /ˌnevə 'maɪnd/
no problem /ˌnəʊ 'prɒbləm/
sorry /'sɒri/
thank you /'θæŋk juː/
thanks /θæŋks/ (informal)
that's OK /'ðæts ˌaʊkeɪ/
you're welcome /ˌjɔː 'welkəm/

## 39 Giving directions

car park /'kɑː ˌpɑːk/
could you tell me the way to /ˌkʊd juː ˌtel miː ðə 'weɪ tə/
go past /ˌgəʊ 'pɑːst/
go straight on /ˌgəʊ 'streɪt ˌɒn/
junction /'dʒʌŋkʃən/
keep going /ˌkiːp 'gəʊɪŋ/
roundabout /'raʊndəˌbaʊt/
take the first on the left /ˌteɪk ðə ˌfɜːst ɒn ðə 'left/
take the second exit /ˌteɪk ðə ˌsekənd 'eksɪt/
take the second on the right /ˌteɪk ðə ˌsekənd ɒn ðə 'raɪt/
traffic lights /'træfɪk ˌlaɪts/
turn left /ˌtɜːn 'left/
turn right /ˌtɜːn 'raɪt/

## 40 On the phone

answering machine /'ɑːnsərɪŋ məˌʃiːn/
Could I speak to ... ? /'kʊd aɪ spiːk tə/
engaged /ɪn'geɪdʒd/
hang up /ˌhæŋ 'ʌp/
Hello /hel'əʊ/
leave a message /ˌliːv ə 'mesɪdʒ/
mobile phone /ˌməʊbaɪl 'fəʊn/
no answer /ˌnəʊ 'ɑːnsə/
pick up the phone /ˌpɪk ʌp ðə 'fəʊn/
public phone /ˌpʌblɪk 'fəʊn/
Who's calling, please? /ˌhuːz 'kɔːlɪŋ ˌpliːz/
wrong number /ˌrɒŋ 'nʌmbə/

## Acknowledgements

I am very grateful to all the schools, institutions, teachers and students around the world who either piloted or commented on the material:

Kristi Alcouffe, Alcouffe Formation, Paris, France
Graham Bathgate, Tokyo, Japan
Katie Head, Cambridge, UK
Magdalena Kijak, Krakow, Poland
Andrea Paul, Melbourne, Australia
Tadeusz Wolanski, Gdansk, Poland

I am also grateful to staff and students at the following institutions who tested the pilot material:

Transfer, Paris, France
IFG Langues, Paris, France
CEL Evry, Evry, France
Ibaraki University, Japan
Simul Academy, Shinjuku School, Tokyo, Japan

I would particularly like to thank Nóirín Burke and Martine Walsh at Cambridge University Press for all their help, guidance and support during the writing of this series. My thanks also to Liz Driscoll for her experienced editing of the material and to Jo Barker and Sarah Warburton for their excellent design and artwork.

# Vocabulary in practice 4

40 units of self-study vocabulary exercises

with tests

Glennis Pye

CAMBRIDGE UNIVERSITY PRESS

# Contents

# To the student

This book will give you the chance to practise your vocabulary in a fun way.

*Vocabulary in Practice 4* has:

- 40 units of short, enjoyable exercises – each unit practises groups of words which belong together
- 4 Tests – one after every 10 units, helping you to remember the words from those units
- an Answer Key
- a Word List – this is a list of all the words in each unit with information about how the words are used.

You can use the book in two ways:

1 Start at the beginning of the book. Do units 1–40 and then do the Tests.
2 Look at the Contents. Do the units you think are important first. When you have finished the book, do the Tests.

You can do each unit in two ways:

1 Do the unit and check your answers in the Answer Key. Study the Word List and learn the words you got wrong. Then do the exercise again.
2 Study the Word List for the unit. Then do the unit and check your answers.

**Note** Do the exercises in this book in pencil. Then you can do the exercises again after a week or a month. Repeating the exercises will help you to remember the words.

Here are some ideas to help you to learn vocabulary:

- Learn groups of words which belong together [e.g. skirt, coat, trousers, etc.].
- Learn a word and also its opposite [e.g. beautiful/ugly, hot/cold].
- Draw pictures: some words are easier to remember if you draw a picture and write the word under it, e.g.

- Write new words in a notebook: write the meaning in English or in your own language, then write a sentence using the word.

I hope you find this book useful and that it makes learning English words fun.

# 1 Family

## A Complete the replies on the right with the words in the box.

| ex-husband ex-wife kids only child orphan partner triplets twins |
|---|

1. She's just had another baby, hasn't she? — That's right. She's got four .................................... now.
2. Do you think you'll have another baby? — Oh yes, I don't want Charlie to be an .................................... .
3. Is Ray her husband? — No, he's her .................................... . They live together, but they're not married.
4. They got divorced three years ago, didn't they? — Yes, Helen's his .................................... .
5. Did you say both his parents were killed during the war? — Yes, he's an .................................... .
6. My sister was born just three minutes after me. — Oh, I didn't realise you two were .................................... .
7. You've got three babies all the same age! — Yes, looking after .................................... is really hard work.
8. We were married, but I divorced him last year. — Oh, he's your .................................... , then.

# 2 People's ages

## A Use the words in the box to write sentences about which gift to buy for each person.

| adult | baby |
|---|---|
| ~~child~~ | teenager |
| toddler | |

1 *Buy the learn-to-write game for Anne-Sophie – she's a child.*
2 ..........
3 ..........
4 ..........
5 ..........

## B Complete the sentences with the words in the box.

| birth | childhood | ~~death~~ | early | late |
|---|---|---|---|---|
| middle-aged | old age | teens | twenties | |

1 (died aged 99) He was 99 at the time of his *death* .
2 (age: 13→19) She was in her .......... when she went abroad for the first time.
3 (age: 37→39) He only got married in his .......... thirties.
4 (age: 50) He's .......... .
5 (age: 0) At the time of my .........., my parents were living in London.
6 (age: 20→29) He learnt to drive when he was in his .......... .
7 (age: 0→12) He had a very happy .......... .
8 (age: 41→43) She was in her .......... forties when she had her third child.
9 (age: 65+) I save money so that I'll be able to live comfortably in my .......... .

# 3 Describing character 1

**A Look at the pictures. Complete Ed and Kate's lists about who they would or would not choose as their new flatmate.**

*Ed*

| *I like* | *I would choose* |
|---|---|
| 1 people who enjoy laughing a lot | Maxine |
| 2 people who always try to do their job well | ............ |
| 3 people who want to be successful | ............ |
| 4 people who are good at learning and understanding things | ............ |

| *I don't like* | *I wouldn't choose* |
|---|---|
| 5 people who think they're better than other people | ............ |
| 6 people who don't talk much | ............ |

Kate

| I like | I would choose |
|---|---|
| 7 people who are relaxed and don't get upset easily | ............ |
| 8 people who are sure they can do things well | ............ |
| 9 people who like to do things to show their love for someone | ............ |
| 10 people who plan things well and don't waste time | ............ |

| I don't like | I wouldn't choose |
|---|---|
| 11 people who don't laugh much | ............ |
| 12 people who never want help, but like to do things themselves | ............ |

Jake – serious, slightly arrogant

Simon – hard-working, very organized

Maxine – has a good sense of humour, easy-going

Jerry – confident, ambitious

Dominic – intelligent, romantic

Lily – quiet, independent

# 4 Describing character 2

## A Find six adjectives for describing character in the grid. Then match the words with the definitions.

| | | | | | | | | | |
|---|---|---|---|---|---|---|---|---|---|
| i | m | m | a | t | u | r | e | t | w |
| x | l | o | z | c | g | e | q | y | c |
| p | s | d | w | r | c | h | d | u | r |
| o | d | e | h | f | h | g | t | i | e |
| m | f | s | t | l | a | f | j | p | a |
| a | r | t | u | n | r | d | n | l | t |
| t | y | y | i | b | m | s | i | k | i |
| u | f | m | d | f | i | z | r | b | v |
| r | e | a | s | o | n | a | b | l | e |
| e | j | n | i | a | g | m | h | o | c |

1 behaving in a silly way, like a younger person ..............................
2 good at using your imagination and thinking of new ideas ..............................
3 very pleasant ..............................
4 fair and showing good judgement ..............................
5 sensible, like an adult ..............................
6 not talking in a proud way about yourself and the good things you have done ..............................

## B Match the words in the box with what the people are saying.

| loyal | optimistic | pessimistic | sensitive | sociable | vain |
|---|---|---|---|---|---|

1 I love spending time with people and meeting new people. ..............................
2 I always support my friends even when they're having difficult times. ..............................
3 I always try to think about how other people feel. ..............................
4 I always think good things are going to happen. ..............................
5 I always think bad things are going to happen. ..............................
6 I look so beautiful, don't I? ..............................

# 5 How you feel

## A Circle the correct word in each sentence.

1 I'm confused / satisfied. Everyone I ask about it tells me something different.

2 I'm very disappointed / nervous. I've got to stand up and talk in front of 300 people.

3 I just feel so depressed / relieved. I have no money, no friends and nowhere to live.

4 I'm frustrated / shocked. A friend of the family has been arrested for murder!

5 I'm so excited / stressed. My best friend is coming and we haven't seen each other for ten years.

6 I'm very homesick / upset. She just suddenly started shouting at me.

## B Complete the sentences with the other words from A.

1 I feel .................................... . I'm very busy at work and I'm studying for an exam in my spare time. I just don't have any time to relax.

2 I feel so .................................... . She really needs my help, but there's nothing I can do.

3 I'm a little .................................... . I haven't seen my friends and family for such a long time.

4 I'm so .................................... you're here. I was beginning to think you'd had an accident.

5 I'm really .................................... . We've had to cancel our skiing holiday because John's broken his leg.

6 I'm not .................................... with the repair work they've done in my house. It's just not good enough.

# 6 Love and marriage

**A Read what the people are saying. Then match the words in the box with the correct person.**

| divorced | married | separated | single | widowed |
|---|---|---|---|---|

1  I'm Patrick. My ex-wife's name is Valerie. ..............................

2  I'm Freya. I'm not married. ..............................

3  I'm Guy. My wife and I don't live together any more. ..............................

4  I'm Lena. My husband's name is Lars. ..............................

5  I'm Jacques. My wife died ten years ago. ..............................

**B Complete the paragraph with the words in the box. Remember to put the verbs in the correct form.**

| an affair | fancy | go out with | live with |
|---|---|---|---|
| relationship | romantic | split up | |

I'd (1) .............................. Kyoko for a long time; I thought she had such beautiful eyes and I loved the way she laughed. When I first met her, she was (2) .............................. someone else. They'd been together for about three years and seemed very happy, so I thought it wasn't likely that their (3) .............................. would end. Then I heard that her boyfriend had been seeing another woman. When Kyoko found out that he'd been having (4) .............................., she told him it was finished and they (5) .............................. . Not long after that, Kyoko and I started seeing each other. Now I'm (6) .............................. her in a flat that we bought together. Next week I'm planning to take her to a restaurant for a (7) .............................. dinner and I'm going to ask her to marry me.

# 7 Your body

## A Circle the correct word on the right for each definition.

| | | |
|---|---|---|
| 1 | the long thing down the centre of your back which supports your body | ribs / (spine) |
| 2 | something which becomes longer or shorter to make a part of your body move and which you can make stronger by doing exercises | heart / muscle |
| 3 | the hair above your eye | eyebrow / eyelashes |
| 4 | the inside part of your hand | palm / spine |
| 5 | the outside part of your whole body | bone / skin |
| 6 | the short hairs that grow from the edge of the part that covers your eye | eyelashes / eyelid |
| 7 | one of the hard pieces in your body | bone / brain |
| 8 | the thing that covers your eye | eyebrow / eyelid |
| 9 | the things in your body that you breathe with | lungs / skin |
| 10 | the thing inside your head that controls how you think and move | brain / palm |
| 11 | the hard curved pieces that surround your chest and protect what is inside your chest | lungs / ribs |
| 12 | the thing in your chest that pumps blood around your body | heart / muscle |

## B Complete the sentences with words from A.

1 She held the insect in the .................... of her hand.

2 One of the players pulled a .................... in his back when he was trying to score a goal.

3 The ball hit him right in the eye and his .................... was badly swollen.

4 The .................... on my face is beginning to get lines on it now that I'm a bit older.

5 It looks like he might need an operation on his .................... to cure his back problem.

6 My sister broke a .................... in her foot when she was playing tennis.

# 8 The senses

## A Complete the word webs with the words in the box.

| hear | listen | look | noise | see | sight | sound | watch |
|---|---|---|---|---|---|---|---|

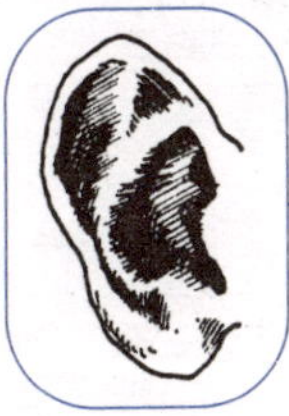

hearing
- noun
  - 1 a s ..............................
  - 2 a ..............................
- verb
  - 3 l ..............................
  - 4 ..............................

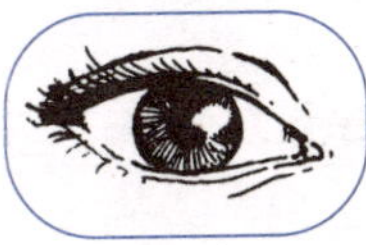

sight
- noun
  - 5 a ..............................
- verb
  - 6 s ..............................
  - 7 l ..............................
  - 8 ..............................

## B The underlined words are in the wrong sentences. Write the correct word for each sentence.

1 Hold your nose so that you can't touch it. ..............................

2 Don't taste that – it'll break. ..............................

3 Smell this – it's really smooth. ..............................

4 This sauce has a really bitter smell. ..............................

5 This jumper smells really smooth. ..............................

6 Feel this – it's really sweet. ..............................

7 Don't drink that water – it feels horrible. ..............................

8 This cheese tastes horrible, but you should try it – it's delicious. ..............................

9 There's a delicious taste of cooking coming from the kitchen. ..............................

# 9 Driving a car

## A The underlined words are in the wrong sentences. Write the correct word for each sentence.

1 The <u>brake</u> is the part of a car that you press with your foot to change gear. ..................

2 The <u>driving test</u> is the part of a car that starts the engine. ..................

3 The <u>accelerator</u> is the part of a car you press with your foot to make it go slower or stop. ..................

4 A <u>clutch</u> is an official document that allows you to drive a car. ..................

5 The <u>ignition</u> is the part of a car that you press with your foot to make it go faster. ..................

6 A <u>driving licence</u> is an official examination that you have to pass to be able to drive. ..................

## B Complete the paragraph with the words in the box.

| change gear | indicate | in first gear | in neutral | move off |
|---|---|---|---|---|
| overtake | park | reverse | slow down | speed up | start up |

Before you switch on the engine, fasten your seatbelt and check that the car is (1) .................. . Now you can (2) .................. the engine by putting the key in the ignition and turning it. Put the car (3) .................. , check in your mirrors to see that no other cars are coming and (4) .................. slowly. (5) .................. by pressing your foot down on the accelerator and remember to (6) .................. . If you want to (7) .................. another car, check in your mirrors and (8) .................. to show that you are moving out. To (9) .................. , press your foot down on the brake. When you arrive at your destination, you should look for somewhere to (10) .................. the car. To do this, it is sometimes easier to (11) .................. the car into the space, but remember to check in your mirrors before you start moving backwards.

# 10 Signs

## A Write the words in the box in the correct place.

| delayed | do not bend | do not disturb | for sale | fragile | no entry |
|---|---|---|---|---|---|
| nothing to declare | on time | out of order | reserved | sale | to let |

1

2

3

£150,000

4

£800/MONTH

5

| FLIGHT | STATUS | FROM | DUE | EXPECTED |
|---|---|---|---|---|
| BA 591 | ______ | MADRID | 16:50 | 16:50 |

6

| FLIGHT | STATUS | FROM | DUE | EXPECTED |
|---|---|---|---|---|
| BA 2363 | ______ | MARSEILLES | 14:35 | 15:15 |

7

8

9

10

11
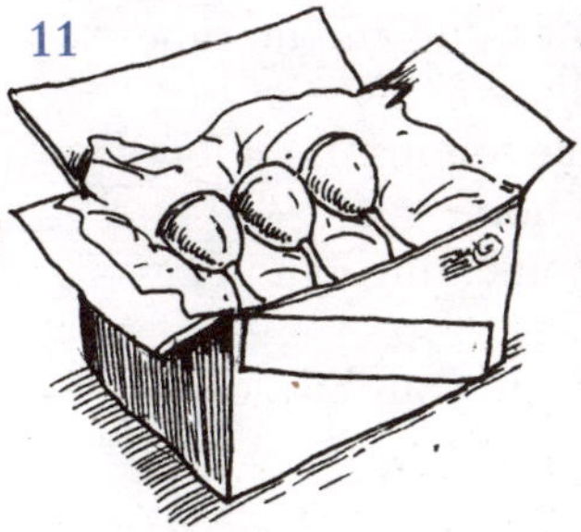

12

# Test 1 (Units 1–10)

**A** **Follow the lines. Then complete what the people are saying.**

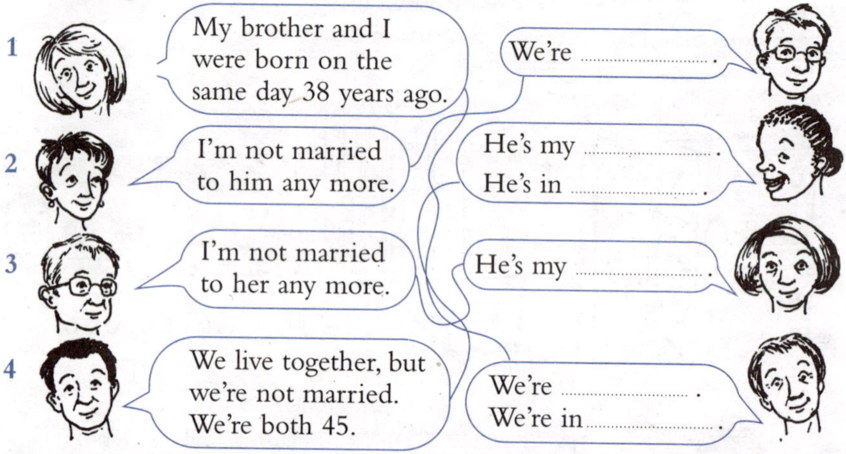


**B** **Read about the people's characters and complete the table.**

**Mike** is very good at learning and understanding things, but sometimes he starts talking about how he thinks he's so much better than everyone else.
**Heather** is very relaxed and doesn't get upset easily, but sometimes she spends too much time looking at herself in the mirror.
**Jack** is great at thinking up new ideas, but then he always thinks bad things are going to happen.

| | **good characteristic** | **bad characteristic** |
|---|---|---|
| **Mike** | ............ | ............ |
| **Heather** | ............ | ............ |
| **Jack** | ............ | ............ . |

**C** **How would you feel if … ?**

**1** you had too much work to do and no time to rest or enjoy yourself ............

**2** you had been in another country for a long time and wanted to go home ............

**3** you kept trying to do something, but just couldn't do it ............

**4** you were five years old and your birthday party was just about to begin ............

# Test 1 (Units 1–10)

## D Label the pictures with words for parts of the body.

1 ..............................
2 ..............................
3 ..............................

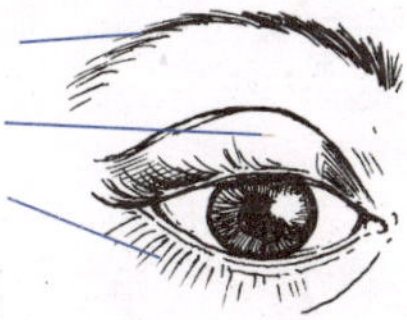

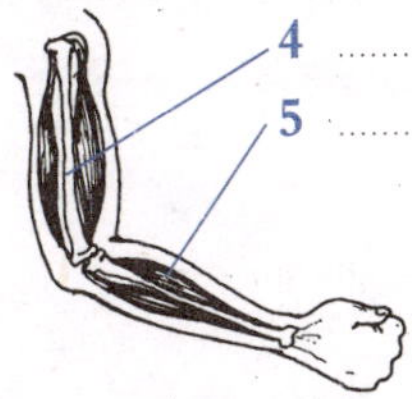

4 ..............................
5 ..............................

## E Complete the sentences with the correct words.

1 You'll have to speak louder. My .............................. isn't too good these days.
2 You go and play. I'll sit here and .............................. you.
3 Stop making that .............................. . I'm trying to think.
4 Can you .............................. the scissors anywhere? I know they're here somewhere.

## F Complete the sentences about driving a car.

1 He's .............................. his car.

2 He's .............................. another car.

3 He's .............................. the car.

4 He's .............................. to turn right.

## G What sign do you see if ... ?

1 something is broken and you cannot use it ..............................

2 a train or plane is not late ..............................

3 a shop is selling things at lower prices than usual ..............................

4 a table in a restaurant is being kept for someone ..............................

# 11 Television

## A Look at the programme schedule. Complete the sentences with the words in the box.

cartoon chat show documentary game show soap opera the news

**5.30 Polly Pet**
One for the little ones – Polly Pet gets into trouble again.

**6.00 The World at Six**
A look at what's been happening at home and abroad.

**7.00 Devon Doorways**
Tonight's episode sees Marcia falling out with just about everyone else in the village.

**8.00 Here and Now**
This week's programme looks at world climate change.

**9.00 In the Chair**
This week's guest is megastar Ben Polance, interviewed by the king of questions.

**9.30 Beginner's Luck**
Who will win the big prize in tonight's challenge?

1 At half past five, there's a ............................ .
2 At six o'clock, there's ............................ .
3 At seven o'clock, there's a ............................ .
4 At eight o'clock, there's a ............................ .
5 At nine o'clock, there's a ............................ .
6 At half past nine, there's a ............................ .

## B Join the people with what they are saying.

1 
*viewer*

2 
*newsreader*

3 
*presenter*

4 
*chat show host*

My first guest tonight is the actor and singer, Joel Williams.

Tonight we are going to look at crime in our cities and what's being done about it.

I'll be back tomorrow with the nine o'clock news, so until then, goodnight.

Now, what shall I watch tonight?

# 12 Cinema

## A Match the pictures with the words in the box.

| action film | animated film | comedy | horror film |
|---|---|---|---|
| science fiction film | thriller | war film | western |

1 ...........................................
2 ...........................................
3 ...........................................
4 ...........................................
5 ...........................................
6 ...........................................
7 ...........................................
8 ...........................................

## B Label the picture with the words in the box.

| actor | actress | cameraman | costume designer | director |
|---|---|---|---|---|
| film star | make-up artist | producer | | |

1 ...........................................
2 ...........................................
3 ...........................................
4 ...........................................
5 ...........................................
6 ...........................................
7 ...........................................
8 ...........................................

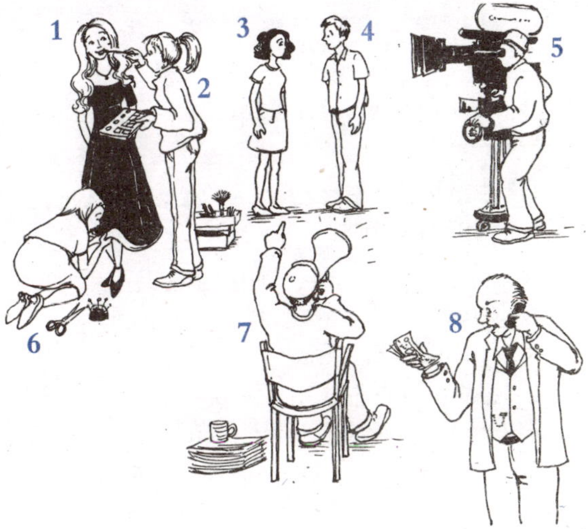

# 13 Newspapers and magazines

## A Read the descriptions and write the words from the box in the word web.

| a broadsheet | ~~a daily~~ | a local newspaper |
| --- | --- | --- |
| a national newspaper | a tabloid | a weekly |

newspaper

- published every day — 1 ........ a daily ........
- news about one area of a country — 2 ................................
- large pages, serious news — 3 ................................
- published once a week — 4 ................................
- news about the whole country — 5 ................................
- small pages, lots of pictures, not much serious news — 6 ................................

## B Match the pairs of sentences.

1 I'm in charge of a newspaper or magazine.

2 I write articles about news.

3 I follow and take photos of famous people.

He's a member of the paparazzi. ☐

She's an editor. ☐

He's a reporter. ☐

## C Find the first letter of each word. Match the words with the definitions.

1 the title of a story printed in large letters on the front of a newspaper ................................

2 a piece of writing ................................

3 newspapers and magazines, or the people who write for them ................................

4 a long piece of writing on a special subject in a newspaper or magazine ................................

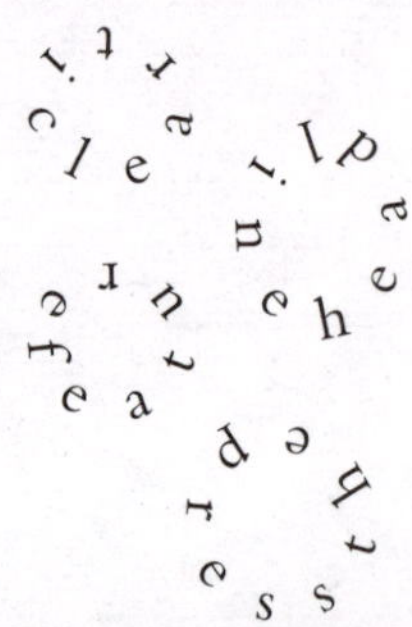

# 14 Books

## A Write the type of book each person should take off the shelf.

1 I'd like to know which museums I should go to see when I'm on holiday. ..................
2 I'm not sure what this word means. ..................
3 I'm not sure how you make apple pie. ..................
4 I'm not sure which countries are next to Poland. ..................
5 I need to find out about what it was like when dinosaurs lived on Earth. ..................
6 I need to do some exercises to improve my English vocabulary. ..................
7 I want to know all about her life. ..................
8 I'm not sure how to load this software. ..................
9 I love reading stories told with pictures. ..................
10 I want to read about something that isn't real. ..................
11 I'd like to know what he thought about all the things that happened to him in his life. ..................

## B The underlined words are in the wrong sentences. Write the correct word for each sentence.

1 A chapter is a book that has a thick, stiff cover. ..................
2 A hardback is a person in a book. ..................
3 A character is one of the parts that a book is divided into. ..................
4 The author of a book is its name. ..................
5 A title is a book that has a thin paper cover. ..................
6 The paperback of a book is the person who has written it. ..................

# 15 Cooking

**A Look at the pictures and complete the sentences. Remember to use the past tense form of the verbs.**

1 I didn't boil the egg. I .................................... it.
2 I didn't fry the chicken. I .................................... it.
3 I didn't bake the peas. I .................................... them.
4 I didn't grill the cake. I .................................... it.
5 I didn't roast the fish. I .................................... it.

**B Circle the correct word in each sentence.**

1

Chop / Peel the onion.

2

Slice / Grate the cheese.

3

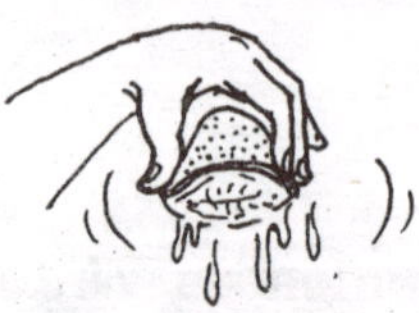

Spread / Squeeze the lemon.

4

Slice / Chop the tomato.

5

Grate / Spread the butter.

6

Peel / Squeeze the potatoes.

# 16 The taste of food

## A Complete what the people are saying with the words in the box.

| bitter sour spicy sweet |
|---|

1

2

3

4

## B Match the plates of food with the people who ate them. Write the letters in the box below.

1 Mine didn't have a very strong taste.

2 There was a lot of salt in mine.

3 Mine tasted great.

4 Mine didn't have any taste at all.

5 There was a lot of cream and butter in mine.

6 Mine tasted really bad.

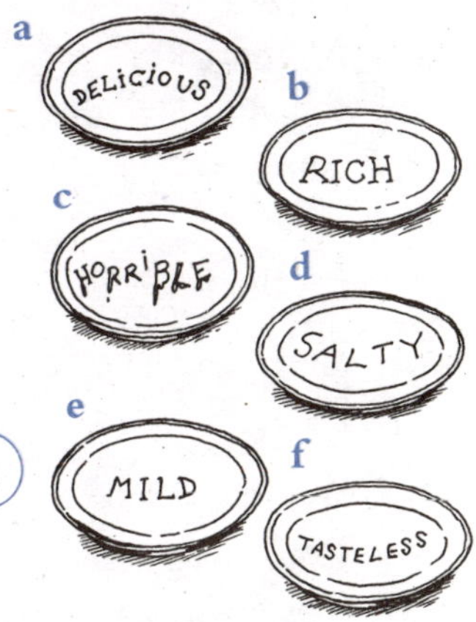


| 1 ............ | 2 ............ | 3 ............ | 4 ............ | 5 ............ | 6 ............ |
|---|---|---|---|---|---|

# 17 Sounds

**A** **Label the pictures with the words in the box.**

| bang | buzz | crackle | creak | crunch | fizz | pop | ring | sizzle | splash |
|---|---|---|---|---|---|---|---|---|---|

1 ……………………
2 ……………………
3 ……………………
4 ……………………
5 ……………………
6 ……………………
7 ……………………
8 ……………………
9 ……………………
10 ……………………

**B** **Complete the sentences with the verbs from A. Remember to use the correct form of the verbs.**

1 Be careful, Jasmine. There's a bee …………………… around your head.
2 Mummy, I'm …………………… you! Are you wet?
3 Listen to how this apple …………………… when I bite into it.
4 The cork …………………… as she opened the champagne.
5 …………………… the bell and see if anyone is at home.
6 Let the sausages …………………… in the pan, turning them until they are brown all over.
7 Can you please stop …………………… that drum – it's giving me a headache.
8 Wait till it stops …………………… before you try to drink it.
9 Don't step on that stair – it …………………… .
10 I love the way the wood …………………… as it burns.

# 18 Home technology

## A Use the words in the box to make new words.

| alarm | camera | clock | control | dish |
|---|---|---|---|---|
| phone | player | player | player | TV |

1 burglar ..............................
2 CD ..............................
3 cordless ..............................
4 digital ..............................
5 DVD ..............................
6 minidisc ..............................
7 radio-alarm ..............................
8 remote ..............................
9 satellite ..............................
10 widescreen ..............................

## B Label the pictures with the new words from A.

1 ..............................
2 ..............................
3 ..............................
4 ..............................
5 ..............................
6 ..............................
7 ..............................
8 ..............................
9 ..............................
10 ..............................

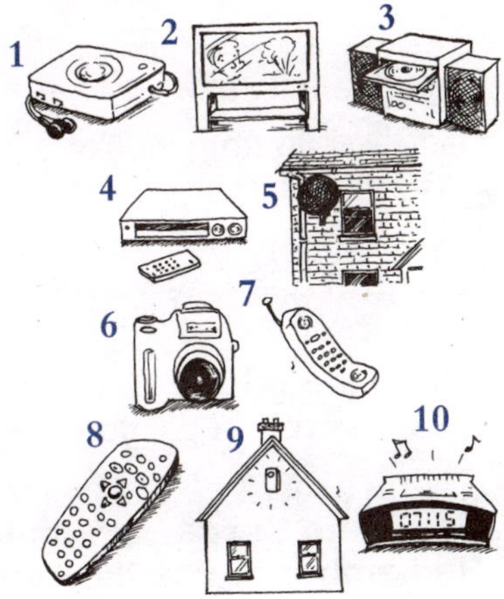


## C Complete the sentences with words from A.

1 This .............................. is great! I can talk into it and walk around the house at the same time.

2 This .............................. is great! The picture and sound quality are excellent.

3 This .............................. is great! I can listen to my music on the train and it's so small it fits in my handbag.

4 This .............................. is great! It wakes me up with music every morning.

5 This .............................. is great! I can delete the awful photos and save the ones I want to keep on my computer.

6 This .............................. is great! I don't have to leave my chair when I want to change channel on the TV.

# 19 The environment

## A Use the words in the box to make new words.

effect fumes layer rain warming waste

1 ozone ..........
2 global ..........
3 greenhouse ..........
4 nuclear ..........
5 exhaust ..........
6 acid ..........

## B Match the new words from A with the definitions.

1 the unwanted gases, etc. that are produced when making nuclear power ..........
2 the gas that comes from a vehicle's engine ..........
3 a type of oxygen around the Earth that stops the sun from harming the Earth ..........
4 water that falls from the sky and contains chemicals that damage plants, etc. ..........
5 the way in which the Earth is slowly getting warmer because gases are stopping heat from leaving it ..........
6 the way in which the Earth's weather is getting warmer because of pollution ..........

## C Complete the paragraph with the words in the box. Remember to use the correct form of the verbs.

organic pesticides pollute pollution recycle recycling

### SAVING OUR ENVIRONMENT

Our environment is in trouble. Modern ways of living and today's industries are (1) .......... it. Most people think there is nothing they can do. This is not true. Everyone can do something to help save our environment. Here's a list of things you can do.

- Help to cut (2) .......... by taking the bus to work instead of your car.
- Buy (3) .......... fruit and vegetables that have not been treated with (4) .......... .
- (5) .......... all your cans, bottles and paper. There should be a (6) .......... centre somewhere near your home, so take them there.

# 20 Natural disasters

## A Label the pictures with the words in the box.

avalanche drought earthquake flood
forest fire hurricane volcanic eruption

1

2

3

4

5

6

7

1 ..................................
2 ..................................
3 ..................................
4 ..................................
5 ..................................
6 ..................................
7 ..................................

## B Complete the paragraph with the words in the box.

casualties death toll rescue operation rescue workers
state of emergency survivors victims

### EARTHQUAKE DISASTER

It is now feared that the (1) .................................. following yesterday's earthquake could be as high as 3,000. Many of the (2) .................................. died when their homes collapsed. The government has declared a (3) .................................. and is organizing a massive (4) .................................. . (5) .................................. are searching for (6) .................................. still trapped under the rubble, although it is now unlikely there will be any more (7) .................................. .

# Test 2 (Units 11–20)

## A Complete the sentences with words for TV programmes and films which mean the same as the words in brackets.

1 I watched a ................................ . (interview with famous actor)

2 I watched a ................................ . (funny film)

3 I watched a ................................ . (people trying to win prizes)

4 I watched a ................................ . (film with cowboys)

5 I watched a ................................ . (very frightening film)

6 I watched a ................................ . (programme with facts about a situation)

## B Complete the sentences with words for newspapers and books.

1 I don't want to read too much serious news when I'm on holiday, so I sometimes buy a ................................ .

2 I'm reading a great ................................ at the moment. It's a story about a woman who starts to imagine she's changing into an animal.

3 We get the ................................ . It's got all sorts of interesting information in it about things that are happening in the area I live in.

4 If you don't know where Majorca is, look it up in an ................................ .

## C Complete the cooking instructions.

1 ................................ an onion and ................................ it into very small pieces. Next, ................................ it in a frying pan in just a little oil.

2 Take some chicken pieces and ................................ some lemon juice over them. Add a little salt and pepper, and ................................ the chicken in the oven for about 45 minutes.

3 Fill a large pan with water. Wait for the water to ................................ before adding the pasta. When the pasta is cooked, pour the sauce onto it and simply ................................ some of your favourite cheese over it.

# Test 2 (Units 11–20)

**D Complete the sentences with words to describe the taste of food.**

1 There's too much lemon in this. It tastes .................................... .

2 There's too much sugar in this. It's too .................................... .

3 There's a lot of pepper in this. It's very .................................... .

4 There aren't many spices in this. It's very .................................... .

5 There's a lot of butter and cream in this. It's very .................................... .

6 There's too much salt in this. It's too .................................... .

**E Circle the correct word for each sentence.**

1 He fizzed / banged / splashed on the door with his fist.
2 The bacon rang / creaked / sizzled in the pan.
3 There was a loud buzz / pop / splash as she landed in the water.
4 The old bed creaked / buzzed / rang as he lay down on it.
5 There was a loud crunch / splash / pop as the tyre burst.

**F Label the pictures with words for home technology.**

1

....................................
....................................

2

....................................
....................................

3

....................................
....................................

4

....................................
....................................

**G Write the words for the definitions.**

1 the people who try to help the people who are affected by a disaster ....................................

2 a storm with very strong winds ....................................

3 damage caused by harmful chemicals to the air, water, etc. ....................................

4 using things again instead of throwing them away ....................................

5 a word which describes food that has not been treated with chemicals ....................................

6 the people who do not die in a disaster ....................................

# 21 Studying at university

## A Complete what the people are saying with the words in the box.

| agriculture | architecture | business studies | engineering | |
|---|---|---|---|---|
| journalism | law | medicine | modern languages | politics |

1 I studied .................................... .

2 I studied .................................... .

3 I studied .................................... .

4 I studied .................................... .

5 I studied .................................... .

6 I studied .................................... .

7 I studied .................................... .

8 I studied .................................... .

9 I studied .................................... .

## B Find the first letter of the words. Match the words with the definitions.

1 someone who is studying at university ....................................

2 someone who teaches at a university ....................................

3 a qualification that you get when you finish university ....................................

4 a talk on a subject given by a teacher at a university to a large group of people ....................................

5 a class at university where a small group of people and their teacher discuss a subject ....................................

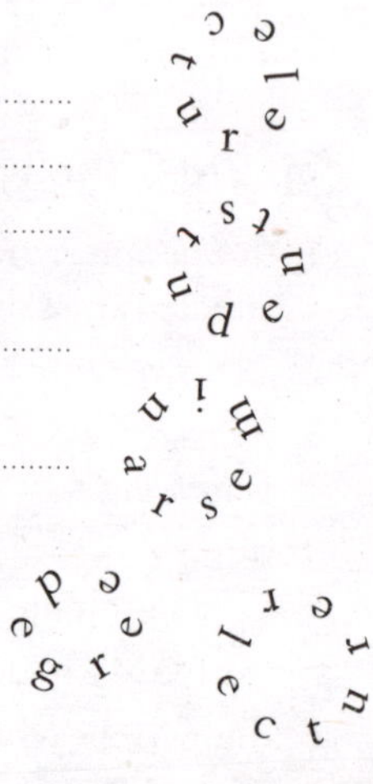

# 22 Crime

## A Match the pairs of sentences. Write the letters in the box below.

1 Jack Jones took things from a shop without paying.
2 Ben Walsh killed someone.
3 Les Bickerton bombed a building because of what he believed in.
4 Kenneth Green got into a house and took all the jewellery.

a He was arrested for murder.
b He was arrested for shoplifting.
c He was arrested for burglary.
d He was arrested for terrorism.

1 ............ 2 ............ 3 ............ 4 ............

## B Complete the sentences about the people in A with the words in the box.

burglar murderer shoplifter terrorist

1 Jack Jones is a .................................... .
2 Ben Walsh is a .................................... .
3 Les Bickerton is a .................................... .
4 Kenneth Green is a .................................... .

## C Complete the paragraph with the words in the box. Remember to put the verbs in the correct form.

arrest burglary break into commit criminals steal victims

### MAN FINALLY CAUGHT

Police investigating the (1) .................................... of ten homes in the Richmond area have (2) .................................... a local man. The man was caught as he (3) .................................... a house in St Margaret's Road. The owner of the house believes he may have been trying to get into the house to (4) .................................... a valuable collection of paintings which she owns. Police think he is likely to be part of a gang of (5).................................... who have been (6) .................................... crimes all over the area recently. PC Kirkland said, 'The (7) .................................... of these crimes often suffer from stress for a long time after the event.'

# 23 Law and justice

## A Label the picture with the words in the box.

court judge jury lawyer

1 ...............................
2 ...............................
3 ...............................
4 ...............................

## B Match the pairs of sentences. Write the letters in the box below.

1 What? They arrested him?

2 Who arrested him?

3 They said they had a witness.

4 I suppose he said he didn't do it.

5 Do they have any other evidence?

6 Do you think he's guilty?

7 30 years?

8 It must be terrible being in prison.

a Well, they said they found some of his hair in her house.

b What? Someone who saw him do it?

c Yes. They took him to the police station to ask him some questions because they think he might have killed her.

d The police, of course.

e Yes, I'm sure he's the one who did it.

f Yes, imagine being kept in a place and not being able to leave.

g Yes, it's long, but that's the sort of sentence you get for murder.

h That's right. He said he was innocent.

1 ........ 2 ........ 3 ........ 4 ........ 5 ........ 6 ........ 7 ........ 8 ........

# 24 Getting a job

## A Circle the word on the right for each definition.

| | | |
|---|---|---|
| 1 | a meeting in which someone asks you questions to see if you are suitable for a job | interview / reference |
| 2 | the money you are paid for doing a job | apply / salary |
| 3 | money your company pays you when you are old and have stopped working for them | pension / salary |
| 4 | a list of printed questions from a company that you answer to try to get a job with them | application form / experience |
| 5 | a car or health insurance, for example, that you get from your company as well as your pay | benefits / CV |
| 6 | an announcement in a newspaper, etc. which invites people to apply for a job | advertisement / interview |
| 7 | something you get when you pass an exam or finish a course of study | benefits / qualifications |
| 8 | a letter written by someone who knows you to say that you are suitable for a job | pension / reference |
| 9 | to officially ask for a job | apply / vacancy |
| 10 | a job that is available for someone to do | advertisement / vacancy |
| 11 | knowledge or skills that you get from doing a job | experience / qualifications |
| 12 | a document with information about jobs you have done and exams you have passed which you send to a company you want to work for | application form / CV |

## B Complete the paragraph with words from A.

**ADMINISTRATION OFFICER**

We have a (1) .................................... for an administration officer to work in our busy Sheffield office. If you have a minimum of two years (2) .................................... in this sort of work and enjoy being part of a team, send for an (3) .................................... to the address below. (4) .................................... is in the region of £12,000, depending on (5) .................................... . (Those with university degrees may receive more.) Other (6) .................................... include the use of the company gym and subsidised meals in the staff restaurant. (7) .................................... will be held on November 5th and 6th at our London office.

# 25 Talking about your work

## A Complete the sentences with the words in the box.

as do for in

1 What do you .................... ?

2 I work .................... a nurse in a large children's hospital.

3 I work .................... a company which sells farm machinery.

4 I work .................... the tourist industry.

## B Complete the paragraphs with the words in the box.

earning employed from home long hours made redundant pay rise permanent promoted set up temporary the office training unemployed

I've been (1) .................................... by my present company for two years now. I came here straight after finishing university. I was really pleased because I was (2) .................................... some money at last. The company has an excellent (3) .................................... programme and so I knew I would learn my job properly. I sometimes have to work (4) .................................... – I didn't get home till after nine o'clock yesterday. But it's possible for me to work (5) .................................... sometimes too – I have a computer in my spare room. It's good to get away from (6) .................................... now and again, and I find I can get a lot done when there's no one else around.

Now that I've been here two years, I'm hoping I'll be (7) .................................... soon – that should also mean I'll get a (8) .................................... and it'd be nice to have a bit more money. In the future I'd like to (9) .................................... my own business, but I'll stay here for now. One of my friends is (10) .................................... at the moment and can't find a job anywhere. He was (11) .................................... last year. Luckily, he's been able to find (12) .................................... work – he's worked for several different companies for a few months each time. But he'd prefer to work for just one and so he's hoping to find a (13) .................................... job very soon.

# 26 Who works in a company

## A Complete what the people are saying with the words in the box.

| accounts manager | boss | chief executive | managing director |
|---|---|---|---|
| personal assistant | personnel manager | receptionist | secretary |
| sales manager | sales representative | | |

1 

I'm Peter Stent. I'm the .................................................. here and I'm in charge of all the people who sell our products.

2 

I'm the .................................................. . I'm responsible for finding people to work for this company.

3 

I'm a .................................................. . I travel around the country selling the company's products. Peter Stent is my.................................................. .

4 

I'm the .................................................. . I'm in charge of all the money the company makes and spends.

5 

I'm Kate Derby, .................................................. and .................................................. . I'm in charge of this company.

6 

I'm a .................................................. . My job is to welcome people as they come into the company's building.

7 

I'm Kate Derby's .................................................. . As head of the company, she's a very busy woman. I arrange all her meetings, make telephone calls and write letters for her, as well as all sorts of other things.

8 

I'm a .................................................. . I do lots of things in my job, such as arranging meetings, making telephone calls and writing letters.

# 27 Money

## A Join the beginnings and endings of the words. Then write the words.

| | |
|---|---|
| 1 bi | ges |
| 2 wa | gage |
| 3 mort | lls |
| 4 re | rest |
| 5 inte | xes |
| 6 ta | nt |

1 ........bills........
2 ..............................
3 ..............................
4 ..............................
5 ..............................
6 ..............................

## B Complete the sentences with the words from A.

1 We all pay .............................. to help pay for schools, hospitals, police officers, etc.
2 I'd like to buy a house, so I need to get a .............................. .
3 I pay £300 .............................. a month for a room in a house that I share with three other people.
4 Don't forget, you'll have .............................. to pay for things like gas and electricity.
5 I have to go to the office every week to collect my .............................. .
6 If you borrow money from the bank, you have to pay them .............................. .

## C Complete the crossword.

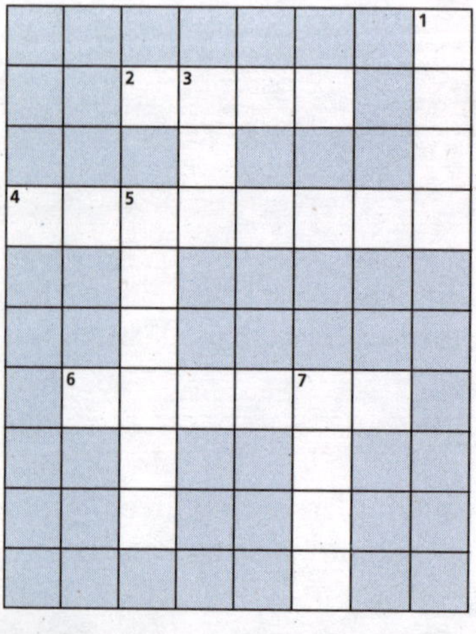

1 money that a company loses
2 having very little money
3 to have to give someone money back because you borrowed money from them
4 money that you spend when you are doing your job that you get back from your company
5 money that a company makes by selling things for more than it cost them to make
6 to have enough money to pay for something
7 having a lot of money

# 28 Using a computer

**A** **Find ten computer words in the grid. Then complete the words in the list.**

| p | d | e | l | e | t | e | g | o | r |
|---|---|---|---|---|---|---|---|---|---|
| a | p | l | m | x | r | p | z | p | q |
| s | h | j | a | c | o | p | y | e | u |
| t | c | u | t | v | e | r | m | n | l |
| e | l | d | a | c | r | b | x | o | s |
| f | o | r | q | e | d | i | t | z | a |
| e | s | p | u | x | c | s | y | n | v |
| y | e | d | r | i | a | i | w | p | e |
| p | r | i | n | t | g | k | l | s | z |

**1** d _ _ _ _ _

**2** o _ _ _

**3** c _ _ _ _

**4** e d _ _

**5** e x _ _

**6** s _ _ _

**7** c _ _ _

**8** p a _ _ _

**9** c _ _

**10** p r _ _ _

**B** **Use words from A to label the computer icons.**

1 

..............................

2 

..............................

3 

..............................

4 

..............................

**C** **Use the words in the box to complete the sentences.**

1 

2 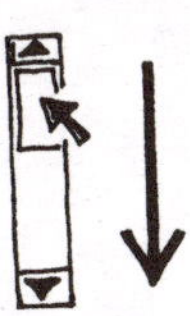

3 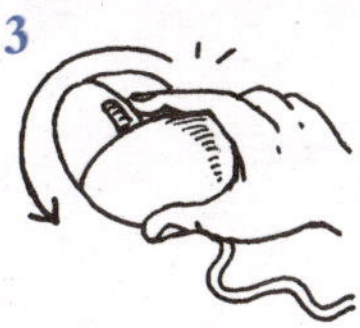

4 

| click | highlight | key | scroll |
|---|---|---|---|

**1** .............................. the words you want to delete.

**2** .............................. down to the end of the page.

**3** .............................. on 'file'.

**4** Press any .............................. .

# 29 Politics

**A** **Complete the definitions with the words in the box.**

| government ministers politicians president / prime minister |
|---|

1 people who represent the country in parliament ..............................

2 the political party that controls the country ..............................

3 the leader of the political party that controls the country ..............................

4 other important people in the political party that controls the country ..............................

**B** **Complete the paragraph with the words in the box. Remember to put the verbs in the correct form.**

| be in power candidates elect hold an election policies political party vote for |
|---|

## HOW WE CHOOSE OUR LEADERS

In a democratic country where the people choose their leaders, this is done by (1) .............................. Everyone in the country can (2) .............................. the person they think would make the best leader. There are usually several (3) .............................. who hope to be (4) .............................. as leader. They try to persuade people to choose them by travelling around the country talking about the things they believe in – about the (5) .............................. they would create if they became leader. Most leaders are members of a (6) .............................. and, when chosen by the people, they will (7) .............................. for a number of years.

# 30 War and peace

## A Look at the picture. Complete the sentences with the words in the box.

| ally | army | civilians | enemy | prisoners |
|---|---|---|---|---|

1 This man is a soldier. He's a member of his country's .................................... .

2 This soldier is fighting against soldier 1. His country is the .................................... of soldier 1's country.

3 This soldier is from another country. He is fighting with soldier 1 against soldier 2. Soldier 3's country is an .................................... of soldier 1's country.

4 These people are .................................... . They have been caught.

5 These people are not soldiers. They are .................................... .

## B Complete the paragraph with the words in the box. Remember to put the verbs in the correct form.

| attack | capture | ceasefire | declare |
|---|---|---|---|
| defend | invade | peace talks | retreat |

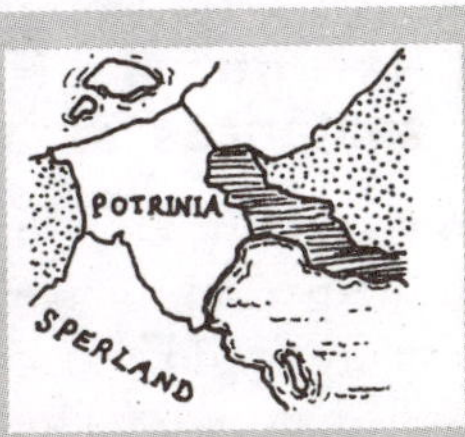


### WAR BETWEEN SPERLAND AND POTRINIA

In the early hours of yesterday morning soldiers from Sperland (1) .................................... Potrinia, despite warnings from the Potrinian government not to come onto their territory. They (2) .................................... villages just across the border. Village leaders were (3) .................................... and taken back to Sperland as prisoners. Villagers tried to (4) .................................... their homes, but few had weapons and most were forced to (5) .................................... to safer areas away from the border. Following these events, Potrinia (6) .................................... war on Sperland. Neighbours of the two countries have called for a (7) .................................... . One said, 'There must be an end to all fighting.' It is hoped that the Sperlish and Potrinian leaders will agree to meet some time next week for (8) .................................... .

# Test 3 (Units 21–30)

## A Complete the sentences with words for university subjects.

1 I want to be a doctor, so I'm going to study .................................... .
2 I want to be a farmer, so I'm going to study .................................... .
3 I want to build roads and bridges, so I'm going to study ............................ .
4 I want to write for a newspaper, so I'm going to study ............................ .
5 I want to teach French and Spanish, so I'm going to study .......................... .
6 I want to be a judge, so I'm going to study .................................... .

## B Match the pairs of sentences. Write the letters in the box below.

1 I steal things from people's houses.
2 I committed a crime because of what I believe in.
3 I decide how long someone should go to prison for.
4 I've committed many crimes.
5 I saw a crime happening.
6 I killed someone.

**a** He's a murderer.
**b** He's a criminal.
**c** He's a burglar.
**d** He's a judge.
**e** He's a witness.
**f** He's a terrorist.

1 .......... 2 .......... 3 .......... 4 .......... 5 .......... 6 ..........

## C Rewrite what Karen is saying about her job. Complete the sentences so that they have the same meaning.

I'm Karen Stirling. I have a job with a large company. I'm the person in charge of all the people who sell the company products. I used to be one of the people who travelled around selling the products, but I was given this better job last year. Some of my friends don't have jobs, so I think I'm very lucky. What's your job?

I'm Karen Stirling. I (1) .............................. a large company. I'm the (2) .............................. . I used to be a (3) .............................. , but I was (4) .............................. last year. Some of my friends are (5) .............................. , so I think I'm very lucky. What do (6) .............................. ?

# Test 3 (Units 21–30)

## D Rewrite what Richard is saying. Complete the sentences so that they have the same meaning.

I'm Richard Moss. I'm at university, but I have just written to a company to get a job. I read about the job in the local newspaper, so I wrote a letter and sent a list of all the qualifications and work experience I have. Now I'm waiting to see if they invite me to a meeting to ask me questions to see if I am suitable for the job. I'd like a good amount of money for the job because I want my own house and will have borrowed money to buy it.

I'm Richard Moss. I'm at university, but I have just (1) .................................... a job with a company. I saw an (2) .................................... for the job in the local newspaper, so I wrote a letter and sent my (3) .................................... . Now I'm waiting to see if I get an (4) .................................... . I'd like a good (5) .................................... because I want my own house and I'll have a (6) .................................... .

## E Put the letters in order to find ten computer words.

1 p y o c ....................................
2 h g i l h i t h g ....................................
3 s t e a p ....................................
4 l o c s r l ....................................
5 i n r p t ....................................
6 v s e a ....................................
7 e t l e d e ....................................
8 d i t e ....................................
9 t u c ....................................
10 t x e i ....................................

## F Write who the people are.

1 I work in politics. ....................................
2 I've been captured by the enemy army. ....................................
3 I'm hoping that people will vote for me. ....................................
4 I'm not a soldier. ....................................
5 I have an important position in the government. ....................................

# 31 Talking about language

## A Complete the sentences with the words in the box.

| accent | adjectives | adverbs | formal | grammar | informal |
|---|---|---|---|---|---|
| nouns | pronunciation | translate | verbs | vocabulary | |

1 You can study .................................. rules from a book, but you can only learn to speak English by speaking.

2 You can use .................................. like 'happily' and 'well' to describe how you do something.

3 My sister doesn't know any English, so I'm going to .................................. the story for her.

4 I find it quite difficult to understand her because she has a very strong Spanish .................................. .

5 It's OK to use .................................. language if you're speaking to a friend.

6 Learning .................................. is very important. If you don't know the correct words, you won't be able to communicate very well.

7 .................................. are words which describe objects or states, like 'dictionary' and 'happiness'.

8 You can use .................................. like 'miserable' and 'smooth' to describe what someone or something is like.

9 .................................. is important – if you can't say a word properly people might not understand you.

10 People usually use more .................................. language when they're in serious situations like interviews.

11 We use .................................. like 'run' and 'smile' to talk about actions.

## B Which question should each person ask? Rewrite what they are saying with the questions in the box.

| What does ... mean? | How do you spell ... ? |
|---|---|
| How do you pronounce ... ? | |

1 I know how to say 'sociable', but I don't know how to write it. ..................................

2 I don't understand the word 'muscle'. ..................................

3 I don't know how to say 'squeeze'. ..................................

# 32 Expressions of time

## A Circle the correct word in each expression of time.

1 at / (for) ages
2 in / now and then
3 no / these days
4 so / these far
5 at / for last
6 no / on longer
7 from / so now on
8 at / from once
9 at / no the moment
10 in / now time
11 on / so time

## B Complete the sentences with the words from A.

1 I don't usually eat sweets, but .................................. I like to have a bar of chocolate.

2 There's a fire – you must leave the building .................................. .

3 If we hurry, we'll be there .................................. to see her before she goes home.

4 I was pleased – the train arrived .................................. , so I wasn't late for my meeting.

5 I'm busy .................................. , but I'll be able to help you when I've finished this.

6 He was 92 years old and could .................................. see or hear very well.

7 We haven't seen them .................................. . We don't seem to be able to find the time to visit each other.

8 I've been trying to do this crossword for three hours and .................................. I've only got one of the answers.

9 .................................. there are millions of cars on the roads. When I was a child, there were far fewer.

10 I promise I won't shout again. .................................. I'll try to be calm and patient.

11 Ah, you're here .................................. . You must have had a difficult journey.

# 33 Everyday objects

**A Put the letters in order to find the words for the things in Mel's bag.**

1 i t e r g h l ..........................................
2 y e k s ..........................................
3 b r l a l m u e ..........................................
4 r i a d y ..........................................
5 a n i t r
m i t e b l e t a ..........................................
6 s o o e l h g c a e n ..........................................
7 l p s t r e a s ..........................................
8 h b r u s ..........................................
9 s s a g l s e ..........................................
10 s r o s c i s s ..........................................
11 s e u t i s s ..........................................

**B Complete the sentences with the words from A.**

1 Mel's got a .............................. to write down all the things she has to do each day.
2 She's got a .............................. to look up the times of her train.
3 She's got a .............................. to light her cigarettes.
4 She's got .............................. to put in the ticket machine at the station.
5 She's got .............................. in case she cuts herself.
6 She's got .............................. in case she needs to blow her nose.
7 She's got a small .............................. in case it rains.
8 She's got her .............................. so that she can read more easily.
9 She's got a .............................. so that she can keep her hair tidy.
10 She's got the .............................. for her flat.
11 She's got .............................. to cut her fingernails.

# 34 Household objects and tools

## A Complete the sentences with the words in the box.

| ashtray | coat hanger | light bulb | tape measure | torch | vase |
|---|---|---|---|---|---|

1 Then all the lights went out and I had to try to find my .................................... .

2 What beautiful flowers, thanks! Let me find a .................................... to put them in.

3 Have you got a .................................... I can hang my jacket on?

4 I don't think you can smoke in here. I can't see an .................................... anywhere.

5 The lamp in the living room isn't working. Where did I put that .................................... I bought the other day?

6 Get the .................................... , so we can see how wide the window is.

## B Look at the pictures. Write the words from the box in the word web.

| drill | hammer | saw | screwdriver |
|---|---|---|---|

tool

1 ....................................

2 ....................................

3 ....................................

4 ....................................

# 35 How good/bad something is

**A** **Find fifteen words in the grid for describing how good or bad something is. Then put the words into the correct group.**

| e | n | t | e | r | t | a | i | n | i | n | g | d |
|---|---|---|---|---|---|---|---|---|---|---|---|---|
| n | s | w | r | t | e | r | r | i | b | l | e | i |
| j | f | o | y | n | b | i | u | b | r | e | f | s |
| o | h | n | u | a | e | n | g | r | e | a | t | a |
| y | k | d | p | i | r | a | n | i | l | c | n | p |
| a | v | e | o | a | w | f | u | l | c | a | b | p |
| b | d | r | e | a | d | f | u | l | s | m | o | o |
| l | p | f | n | m | u | h | g | i | z | u | r | i |
| e | y | u | l | y | l | n | c | a | j | s | i | n |
| g | r | l | d | h | l | m | k | n | g | i | n | t |
| h | i | n | t | e | r | e | s | t | i | n | g | i |
| j | w | z | e | x | c | i | t | i | n | g | z | n |
| k | v | f | a | s | c | i | n | a | t | i | n | g |

**good:** ..............., ..............., ...............,
..............., ..............., ...............,
..............., ..............., ................

**bad:** ..............., ..............., ...............,
..............., ..............., ................

**B** **The <u>underlined</u> words are in the wrong sentences. Write the correct word for each sentence.**

1 Her speech was so <u>interesting</u> I almost fell asleep. ...............

2 I thought lots of people would be there, but hardly anyone came. It was very <u>amusing</u>. ...............

3 It's a very <u>disappointing</u> book. You can learn a lot from it. ...............

4 The film was really <u>exciting</u>. I laughed a lot. ...............

5 First we missed our flight and then two days after we arrived I broke my leg! It was a <u>boring</u> holiday. ...............

6 Riding down the hill was so <u>terrible</u>. I've never been that fast on my bike before. ...............

# 36 Describing objects

## A Complete the sentences with the words in the box. Then join the objects with the sentences.

| made of | stuff | thing | use for | use to |
|---|---|---|---|---|

1 

I'd like to buy some .................................... to wash my hair with.

2 

I'd like to buy a .................................... for opening bottles of wine.

3 

I'd like to buy one of those things you .................................... cutting the grass.

4 

I'd like to buy one of those things you .................................... clean the kitchen floor.

5 

I'd like to buy some of those things that are .................................... paper and that you blow your nose on.

## B What are the objects made of? Match the words in the box with the groups of objects.

| cardboard | glass | leather | material | ~~metal~~ |
|---|---|---|---|---|
| paper | plastic | rubber | wood | |

1 ......*metal*......
a car
a knife
scissors

2 ....................................
a letter
an envelope
a magazine

3 ....................................
a dress
a towel
curtains

4 ....................................
a birthday card
a box for chocolates
a book cover

5 ....................................
a comb
a computer keyboard
a baby's bottle

6 ....................................
a table
a baseball bat
a fence

7 ....................................
a window
a light bulb
a beer bottle

8 ....................................
a wallet
a handbag
a belt

9 ....................................
a tyre
gloves for washing up
a ball

# 37 Using your eyes

## A Circle the correct word in each pair.

1

gaze / wink

2

examine / glance

3

frown / look at

4

blink / peep

5

look for / stare

6

glare / squint

## B Complete the sentences with the other words from A. Remember to put the verbs in the correct form.

1 Don't .................................... at people. It's not very polite.

2 She quickly .................................... around the room to see if she knew anyone there.

3 He blew on her face, making her .................................... .

4 He sat .................................... out of the window, thinking about when he might see her again.

5 She .................................... at him. She was so angry about what he had done.

6 Here, .................................... this photograph – it's me when I was five years old.

# 38 Ways of walking

**A Find the words for ten ways of walking in the grid. Then complete the words in the list.**

| p | a | d | d | l | e | c | q | e | n |
|---|---|---|---|---|---|---|---|---|---|
| b | n | o | m | i | j | r | p | s | j |
| d | e | s | k | i | p | a | w | l | v |
| g | r | t | s | z | g | w | l | i | h |
| l | h | c | l | i | k | l | c | p | n |
| i | k | b | c | b | h | m | e | i | n |
| m | m | a | r | c | h | t | h | o | p |
| p | q | a | e | s | t | r | o | l | l |
| i | s | w | e | u | f | i | m | k | h |
| l | t | v | p | f | l | p | y | r | t |

1 cra ..........................
2 cre ..........................
3 h ..........................
4 l ..........................
5 m ..........................
6 p ..........................
7 sk ..........................
8 sl ..........................
9 st ..........................
10 t ..........................

**B Label the pictures with five of the words from A.**

1

..................................

2

..................................

3

..................................

4

..................................

5

..................................

**C Match the definitions with the other five words from A.**

1 to walk somewhere in a slow, relaxed way ..................................
2 to walk very quietly and carefully ..................................
3 to move about by jumping up and down on one foot ..................................
4 to walk with difficulty because one of your legs or feet is hurt ..................................
5 to move forwards by jumping quickly on one foot then the other and lifting your knees high ..................................

# 39 Phrasal verbs

## A Match the words in the box with the pictures.

| Calm down! | Cheer up! | Come on! |
|---|---|---|
| Hang on! | Slow down! | Speed up! |

1

2

3

4

5

6

## B Complete the sentences with the words in the box.

make   pick   put   take

1 If you don't like the situation, don't just .................................... up with it. Do something to change it.

2 My train gets in at 17.30. Will you be able to .................................... me up or should I get a taxi to your house?

3 Don't believe everything they tell you. They .................................... up stories all the time.

4 I want something to do in my spare time, so I've decided to .................................... up golf.

# 40 Giving your opinion

## A Put the expressions in the box into three groups.

as far as I'm concerned   I believe in   I have my doubts about
I'm against   I'm in favour of   in my opinion
in my view   to my mind

**expressing your opinion**

.................................................. ..................................................

.................................................. ..................................................

**positive opinion** **negative opinion**

.................................................. ..................................................

.................................................. ..................................................

## B Read the sentences. Then rewrite them with the other four expressions from A.

**1** In my opinion, parking charges should be higher.
As ..................................................................................................

**2** In my view, there should be more cycle tracks.
To ..................................................................................................

**3** I have my doubts about reducing bus fares.
..................................................................................................

**4** I believe in increasing speed limits on motorways.
..................................................................................................

## C Complete the conversations with the words in the box.

about   agree   disagree   of   think   view

Jane: What do you think (1) ........................ his latest film?
Lawrence: I (2) ........................ it's really great.
Holly: Oh no, I (3) ........................ . The one he made last year was much better.

Steven: What do you think (4) ........................ moving to a different office?
Millie: Well, it's only my point of (5) ........................ , but I'd prefer to stay here.
Vivien: Yes, I (6) ........................ . I'd rather stay here too.

# Test 4 (Units 31–40)

## A Complete the sentences.

1 The words 'tree', 'computer' and 'enemy' are all .................................... .

2 The words 'feel', 'fry' and 'arrest' are all .................................... .

3 The words 'arrogant', 'romantic' and 'delicious' are all .................................... .

4 The words 'quickly', 'slowly' and 'happily' are all .................................... .

## B Write another time expression which means the same.

1 for a very long time ..............................  4 not any more ..............................

2 not very often ..............................  5 up till now ..............................

3 not early and not late ..............................  6 right now ..............................

## C Complete the sentences to describe the objects.

1 
2 
3 
4 

1 This .............................. is made of .............................. and you .............................. it .............................. hold flowers.

2 These .............................. are made of .............................. and you .............................. them .............................. blow your nose.

3 These .............................. are made of .............................. and you .............................. them .............................. cutting things.

4 This .............................. is made of .............................. and you .............................. it .............................. finding out how big something is.

## D Put the words in the box in three groups.

| awful boring brilliant disappointing dreadful dull great terrible wonderful |
|---|

| **very bad** | **very good** | **not interesting** |
|---|---|---|
| .............................. | .............................. | .............................. |
| .............................. | .............................. | .............................. |
| .............................. | .............................. | .............................. |

# Test 4 (Units 31–40)

## E The underlined words are in the wrong sentences. Write the correct word for each sentence.

1 He's <u>limping</u> because the sun's in his eyes. ..............................

2 She's <u>peeping</u> in the water. ..............................

3 He's <u>creeping</u> through the hole to see what's there. ..............................

4 He's <u>paddling</u> up the stairs because he doesn't want anyone to hear him. ..............................

5 She's <u>blinking</u> because she's confused. ..............................

6 He's <u>frowning</u> because he's hurt his leg. ..............................

## F Write a phrasal verb for each definition.

1 become happy after being sad ..............................

2 wait ..............................

3 collect ..............................

4 go slower ..............................

5 start doing a sport or hobby ..............................

6 go faster ..............................

## G Put the words in order to make sentences.

1 far it's right not as I'm as concerned

..............................................................................................

2 think you what about do it?

..............................................................................................

3 favour in it of I'm

..............................................................................................

4 my in it's wrong opinion

..............................................................................................

5 it against I'm

..............................................................................................

# Answer Key

## 1 Family

**A** 1 kids
2 only child
3 partner
4 ex-wife
5 orphan
6 twins
7 triplets
8 ex-husband

## 2 People's ages

**A** 1 *Buy the learn-to-write game for Anne-Sophie – she's a child.*
2 Buy the rattle for Gianni – he's a baby.
3 Buy the tricycle for Melanie – she's a toddler.
4 Buy the trainers for Nicola – she's a teenager.
5 Buy the theatre tickets for Gary – he's an adult.

**B** 1 *death*
2 teens
3 late
4 middle-aged
5 birth
6 twenties
7 childhood
8 early
9 old age

## 3 Describing character 1

**A** 1 *Maxine*
2 Simon
3 Jerry
4 Dominic
5 Jake
6 Lily
7 Maxine
8 Jerry
9 Dominic
10 Simon
11 Jake
12 Lily

## 4 Describing character 2

**A** 1 immature
2 creative
3 charming
4 reasonable
5 mature
6 modest

**B** 1 sociable
2 loyal
3 sensitive
4 optimistic
5 pessimistic
6 vain

## 5 How you feel

**A** 1 confused
2 nervous
3 depressed
4 shocked
5 excited
6 upset

**B** 1 stressed
2 frustrated
3 homesick
4 relieved
5 disappointed
6 satisfied

## 6 Love and marriage

**A** 1 divorced
2 single
3 separated
4 married
5 widowed

**B** 1 fancied
2 going out with
3 relationship
4 an affair
5 split up
6 living with
7 romantic

## 7 Your body

**A** **1** *spine*
**2** muscle
**3** eyebrow
**4** palm
**5** skin
**6** eyelashes
**7** bone
**8** eyelid
**9** lungs
**10** brain
**11** ribs
**12** heart

**B** **1** palm
**2** muscle
**3** eyelid
**4** skin
**5** spine
**6** bone

## 8 The senses

**A** **1** a sound
**2** a noise
**3** listen
**4** hear
**5** a sight
**6** see
**7** look
**8** watch

**B** **1** smell
**2** touch
**3** Feel
**4** taste
**5** feels
**6** Taste
**7** tastes
**8** smells
**9** smell

## 9 Driving a car

**A** **1** clutch
**2** ignition
**3** brake
**4** driving licence
**5** accelerator
**6** driving test

**B** **1** in neutral
**2** start up
**3** in first gear
**4** move off
**5** Speed up
**6** change gear
**7** overtake
**8** indicate
**9** slow down
**10** park
**11** reverse

## 10 Signs

**A** **1** out of order
**2** do not disturb
**3** for sale
**4** to let
**5** on time
**6** delayed
**7** nothing to declare
**8** reserved
**9** no entry
**10** do not bend
**11** fragile
**12** sale

## Test 1 (Units 1–10)

**A** **1** twins, our late thirties
**2** divorced
**3** ex-husband
**4** partner, his forties

**B** **Mike** intelligent, arrogant
**Heather** easy-going, vain
**Jack** creative, pessimistic

**C** **1** stressed
**2** homesick
**3** frustrated
**4** excited

**D** **1** eyebrow
**2** eyelid
**3** eyelashes
**4** bone
**5** muscle

...ng
...tch
**3** noise
**4** see

**F** **1** parking
**2** overtaking
**3** reversing
**4** indicating

**G** **1** out of order
**2** on time
**3** sale
**4** reserved

## 11 Television

**A** 1 cartoon
2 the news
3 soap opera
4 documentary
5 chat show
6 game show

**B** 1 Now, what shall I watch tonight?
2 I'll be back tomorrow with the nine o'clock news, so until then, goodnight.
3 Tonight we are going to look at crime in our cities and what's being done about it.
4 My first guest tonight is the actor and singer, Joel Williams.

## 12 Cinema

**A** 1 science fiction film
2 thriller
3 war film
4 horror film
5 western
6 action film
7 animated film
8 comedy

**B** 1 film star
2 make-up artist
3 actress
4 actor
5 cameraman
6 costume designer
7 director
8 producer

## 13 Newspapers and magazines

**A** 1 *a daily*
2 a local newspaper
3 a broadsheet
4 a weekly
5 a national newspaper
6 a tabloid

**B** 1 She's an editor.
2 He's a reporter.
3 He's a member of the paparazzi.

**C** 1 headline
2 article
3 the press
4 feature

## 14 Books

**A** 1 guidebook
2 dictionary
3 cookery book
4 atlas
5 encyclopedia
6 textbook
7 biography
8 computer manual
9 comic
10 novel
11 autobiography

**B** 1 hardback
2 character
3 chapter
4 title
5 paperback
6 author

## 15 Cooking

**A** 1 fried
2 roasted
3 boiled
4 baked
5 grilled

**B** 1 Chop
2 Grate
3 Squeeze
4 Slice
5 Spread
6 Peel

## 16 The taste of food

**A**
1 spicy
2 bitter
3 sweet
4 sour

**B**
1 e
2 d
3 a
4 f
5 b
6 c

## 17 Sounds

**A**
1 buzz
2 splash
3 crunch
4 pop
5 ring
6 sizzle
7 bang
8 fizz
9 creak
10 crackle

**B**
1 buzzing
2 splashing
3 crunches
4 popped
5 Ring
6 sizzle
7 banging
8 fizzing
9 creaks
10 crackles

## 18 Home technology

**A**
1 burglar alarm
2 CD player
3 cordless phone
4 digital camera
5 DVD player
6 minidisc player
7 radio-alarm clock
8 remote control
9 satellite dish
10 widescreen TV

**B**
1 minidisc player
2 widescreen TV
3 CD player
4 DVD player
5 satellite dish
6 digital camera
7 cordless phone
8 remote control
9 burglar alarm
10 radio-alarm clock

**C**
1 cordless phone
2 widescreen TV
3 minidisc player
4 radio-alarm clock
5 digital camera
6 remote control

## 19 The environment

**A**
1 ozone layer
2 global warming
3 greenhouse effect
4 nuclear waste
5 exhaust fumes
6 acid rain

**B**
1 nuclear waste
2 exhaust fumes
3 ozone layer
4 acid rain
5 greenhouse effect
6 global warming

**C**
1 polluting
2 pollution
3 organic
4 pesticides
5 Recycle
6 recycling

## 20 Natural disasters

**A**
1 flood
2 earthquake
3 forest fire
4 hurricane
5 volcanic eruption
6 drought
7 avalanche

**B**
1 death toll
2 victims
3 state of emergency
4 rescue operation
5 Rescue workers
6 casualties
7 survivors

## Test 2 (Units 11–20)

**A** 1 chat show
2 comedy
3 game show
4 western
5 horror film
6 documentary

**B** 1 tabloid
2 novel
3 local newspaper
4 atlas

**C** 1 Peel, chop, fry
2 squeeze, roast
3 boil, grate

**D** 1 bitter
2 sweet
3 spicy
4 mild
5 rich
6 salty

**E** 1 banged
2 sizzled
3 splash
4 creaked
5 pop

**F** 1 remote control
2 burglar alarm
3 satellite dish
4 radio-alarm clock

**G** 1 rescue workers
2 hurricane
3 pollution
4 recycling
5 organic
6 survivors

## 21 Studying at university

**A** 1 law
2 medicine
3 politics
4 business studies
5 agriculture
6 architecture
7 engineering
8 modern languages
9 journalism

**B** 1 student
2 lecturer
3 degree
4 lecture
5 seminar

## 22 Crime

**A** 1 b
2 a
3 d
4 c

**B** 1 shoplifter
2 murderer
3 terrorist
4 burglar

**C** 1 burglary
2 arrested
3 broke into
4 steal
5 criminals
6 committing
7 victims

## 23 Law and justice

**A** 1 judge
2 court
3 jury
4 lawyer

**B** 1 c
2 d
3 b
4 h
5 a
6 e
7 g
8 f

## 24 Getting a job

**A** 1 interview
2 Salary
3 pension
4 application form
5 benefits
6 advertisement
7 qualifications
8 reference
9 apply
10 vacancy
11 experience
12 CV

**B** 1 vacancy
2 experience
3 application form
4 salary
5 qualifications
6 benefits
7 Interviews

## 25 Talking about your work

**A** **1** do
**2** as
**3** for
**4** in

**B** **1** employed
**2** earning
**3** training
**4** long hours
**5** from home
**6** the office
**7** promoted
**8** pay rise
**9** set up
**10** unemployed
**11** made redundant
**12** temporary
**13** permanent

## 26 Who works in a company

**A** **1** sales manager
**2** personnel manager
**3** sales representative, boss
**4** accounts manager
**5** chief executive, managing director
**6** receptionist
**7** personal assistant
**8** secretary

## 27 Money

**A** **1** *bills*
**2** wages
**3** mortgage
**4** rent
**5** interest
**6** taxes

**B** **1** taxes
**2** mortgage
**3** rent
**4** bills
**5** wages
**6** interest

**C** **1** loss
**2** poor
**3** owe
**4** expenses
**5** profit
**6** afford
**7** rich

## 28 Using a computer

**A** **1** delete
**2** open
**3** close
**4** edit
**5** exit
**6** save
**7** copy
**8** paste
**9** cut
**10** print

**B** **1** open
**2** copy
**3** print
**4** save

**C** **1** Highlight
**2** Scroll
**3** Click
**4** key

## 29 Politics

**A** **1** politicians
**2** government
**3** president / prime minister
**4** ministers

**B** **1** holding an election
**2** vote for
**3** candidates
**4** elected
**5** policies
**6** political party
**7** be in power

## 30 War and peace

**A** **1** army
**2** enemy
**3** ally
**4** prisoners
**5** civilians

**B** **1** invaded
**2** attacked
**3** captured
**4** defend
**5** retreat
**6** declared
**7** ceasefire
**8** peace talks

## Test 3 (Units 21–30)

**A**
1 medicine
2 agriculture
3 engineering
4 journalism
5 modern languages
6 law

**B**
1 c
2 f
3 d
4 b
5 e
6 a

**C**
1 work for
2 sales manager
3 sales representative
4 promoted
5 unemployed
6 you do

**D**
1 applied for
2 advertisement
3 CV
4 interview
5 salary
6 mortgage

**E**
1 copy
2 highlight
3 paste
4 scroll
5 print
6 save
7 delete
8 edit
9 cut
10 exit

**F**
1 politician
2 prisoner
3 candidate
4 civilian
5 minister

## 31 Talking about language

**A**
1 grammar
2 adverbs
3 translate
4 accent
5 informal
6 vocabulary
7 Nouns
8 adjectives
9 Pronunciation
10 formal
11 verb

**B**
1 How do you spell 'sociable'?
2 What does 'muscle' mean?
3 How do you pronounce 'squeeze'?

## 32 Expressions of time

**A**
1 for
2 now
3 these
4 so
5 at
6 no
7 from
8 at
9 at
10 in
11 on

**B**
1 now and then
2 at once
3 in time
4 on time
5 at the moment
6 no longer
7 for ages
8 so far
9 These days
10 From now on
11 at last

## 33 Everyday objects

**A**
1 lighter
2 keys
3 umbrella
4 diary
5 train timetable
6 loose change
7 plasters
8 brush
9 glasses
10 scissors
11 tissues

**B**
1 diary
2 train timetable
3 lighter
4 loose change
5 plasters
6 tissues
7 umbrella
8 glasses
9 brush
10 keys
11 scissors

## 34 Household objects and tools

**A** **1** torch
**2** vase
**3** coat hanger
**4** ashtray
**5** light bulb
**6** tape measure

**B** **1** screwdriver
**2** drill
**3** saw
**4** hammer

## 35 How good/bad something is

**A** **good**
amusing
brilliant
enjoyable
entertaining
exciting
fascinating
great
interesting
wonderful

**bad**
awful
boring
disappointing
dreadful
dull
terrible

**B** **1** boring
**2** disappointing
**3** interesting
**4** amusing
**5** terrible
**6** exciting

## 36 Describing objects

**A** **1** thing
**2** made of
**3** stuff
**4** use for
**5** use to

**B** **1** *metal*
**2** paper
**3** material
**4** cardboard
**5** plastic
**6** wood
**7** glass
**8** leather
**9** rubber

## 37 Using your eyes

**A** **1** wink
**2** examine
**3** frown
**4** peep
**5** look for
**6** squint

**B** **1** stare
**2** glanced
**3** blink
**4** gazing
**5** glared
**6** look at

## 38 Ways of walking

**A** **1** crawl
**2** creep
**3** hop
**4** limp
**5** march
**6** paddle
**7** skip
**8** slip
**9** stroll
**10** trip

**B** **1** march
**2** crawl
**3** slip
**4** paddle
**5** trip

**C** **1** stroll
**2** creep
**3** hop
**4** limp
**5** skip

## 39 Phrasal verbs

**A** 1 Cheer up!
2 Slow down!
3 Come on!
4 Speed up!
5 Calm down!
6 Hang on!

**B** 1 put
2 pick
3 make
4 take

## 40 Giving your opinion

**A** **expressing your opinion**
as far as I'm concerned
in my opinion
in my view
to my mind
**positive opinion**
I believe in
I'm in favour of
**negative opinion**
I have my doubts about
I'm against

**B** 1 As far as I'm concerned, parking charges should be higher.
2 To my mind, there should be more cycle tracks.
3 I'm against reducing bus fares.
4 I'm in favour of increasing speed limits on motorways.

**C** 1 of
2 think
3 disagree
4 about
5 view
6 agree

## Test 4 (Units 31–40)

**A** 1 nouns
2 verbs
3 adjectives
4 adverbs

**B** 1 for ages
2 now and then
3 on time
4 no longer
5 so far
6 at once

**C** 1 vase, glass, use, to
2 tissues, paper, use, to
3 scissors, metal, use, for
4 tape measure, plastic, use, for

**D** **very bad**
awful, dreadful, terrible
**very good**
brilliant, great, wonderful
**not interesting**
boring, disappointing, dull

**E** 1 blinking
2 paddling
3 peeping
4 creeping
5 frowning
6 limping

**F** 1 cheer up
2 hang on
3 pick up
4 slow down
5 take up
6 speed up

**G** 1 As far as I'm concerned, it's not right.
2 What do you think about it?
3 I'm in favour of it.
4 In my opinion, it's wrong.
5 I'm against it.

# Word List

The words in this list are British English. Sometimes we give you an important American English word which means the same.

## 1 Family

ex-husband /ˌeks hʌzbənd/
ex-wife /ˌeks'waɪf/
kids /kɪdz/ (informal)
only child /ˌəʊnli 'tʃaɪld/
orphan /'ɔːfən/
partner /'pɑːtnə/
triplets /'trɪpləts/
twins /twɪnz/

## 2 People's ages

adult /'ædʌlt/
baby /'beɪbi/
birth /bɜːθ/
child /tʃaɪld/ (plural = children)
childhood /'tʃaɪldhʊd/
death /deθ/
in your teens /ɪn jɔː 'tiːnz/
in your twenties /ɪn jɔː 'twentiz/
late twenties /ˌleɪt 'twentiz/
early thirties /ˌɜːli 'θɜːtiz/
middle-aged /ˌmɪdl'eɪdʒd/
old age /ˌəʊld 'eɪdʒ/
teenager /'tiːnˌeɪdʒə/
toddler /'tɒdlə/

## 3 Describing character 1

ambitious /æm'bɪʃəs/
arrogant /'ærəgənt/
confident /'kɒnfɪdənt/
easy-going /ˌiːzi'gəʊɪŋ/
hard-working /ˌhɑːd'wɜːkɪŋ/
have a good sense of humour /hæv ə ˌgʊd ˌsens əv 'hjuːmə/

independent /ˌɪndɪ'pendənt/
intelligent /ɪn'telɪdʒənt/
organized /'ɔːgənaɪzd/
quiet /kwaɪət/
romantic /rə'mæntɪk/
serious /'sɪəriəs/

## 4 Describing character 2

charming /'tʃɑːmɪŋ/
creative /kri'eɪtɪv/
immature /ˌɪmə'tjʊə/
loyal /lɔɪəl/
mature /mə'tjʊə/
modest /'mɒdɪst/
optimistic /ˌɒptɪ'mɪstɪk/
pessimistic /ˌpesɪ'mɪstɪk/
reasonable /'riːzənəbl/
sensitive /'sensɪtɪv/
sociable /'səʊʃəbl/
vain /veɪn/

## 5 How you feel

confused /kən'fjuːzd/
depressed /dɪ'prest/
disappointed /ˌdɪsə'pɔɪntɪd/
excited /ɪk'saɪtɪd/
frustrated /frʌs'treɪtɪd/
homesick /'həʊmsɪk/
nervous /'nɜːvəs/
relieved /rɪ'liːvd/
satisfied /'sætɪsfaɪd/
shocked /ʃɒkt/
stressed /strest/
upset /ʌp'set/

## 6 Love and marriage

affair /ə'feə/
divorced /dɪ'vɔːst/
fancy /'fænsi/ (informal)
go out with /ˌgəʊ 'aʊt wɪð/ (*past tense* went, *past participle* gone)
live with /'lɪv wɪð/
married /'mærid/
relationship /rɪ'leɪʃənʃɪp/
romantic /rə'mæntɪk/
separated /'sepəreɪtɪd/
single /'sɪŋgl/
split up /ˌsplɪt 'ʌp/ (*past tense* & *past participle* split)
widowed /'wɪdəʊd/

## 7 Your body

bone /bəʊn/
brain /breɪn/
eyebrow /'aɪbraʊ/
eyelashes /'aɪlæʃɪz/
eyelid /'aɪlɪd/
heart /hɑːt/
lungs /lʌŋz/
muscle /'mʌsl/
palm /pɑːm/
ribs /rɪbz/
skin /skɪn/
spine /spaɪn/

## 8 The senses

feel /fiːl/ (*past tense* & *past participle* felt)
hear /hɪə/ (*past tense* & *past participle* heard)
hearing /'hɪərɪŋ/
listen /'lɪsən/
look /lʊk/
noise /nɔɪz/
see /siː/ (*past tense* saw, *past participle* seen)
sight /saɪt/
smell /smel/ (*past tense* & *past participle* smelt *or* smelled)

sound /saʊnd/
taste /teɪst/
touch /tʌtʃ/
watch /wɒtʃ/

## 9 Driving a car

accelerator /ək'seləreɪtə/
brake (noun) /breɪk/
change gear /ˌtʃeɪndʒ 'gɪə/
clutch /klʌtʃ/
driving licence /'draɪvɪŋ ˌlaɪsəns/
driving test /'draɪvɪŋ ˌtest/
ignition /ɪg'nɪʃən/
indicate /'ɪndɪkeɪt/
in first gear /ɪn ˌfɜːst 'gɪə/
in neutral /ɪn 'njuːtrəl/
move off /ˌmuːv 'ɒf/
overtake /ˌəʊvə'teɪk/
park /pɑːk/
reverse /rɪ'vɜːs/
slow down /ˌsləʊ 'daʊn/
speed up /ˌspiːd 'ʌp/
start up /ˌstɑːt 'ʌp/

## 10 Signs

delayed /dɪ'leɪd/
do not bend /ˌduː nɒt 'bend/
do not disturb /ˌduː nɒt dɪ'stɜːb/
for sale /fə 'seɪl/
fragile /'frædʒaɪl/
no entry /ˌnəʊ 'entri/
nothing to declare /ˌnʌθɪŋ təː dɪ'kleə/
on time /ˌɒn taɪm/
out of order /ˌaʊt əv 'ɔːdə/
reserved /rɪ'zɜːvd/
sale /seɪl/
to let /təː 'let/

## 11 Television

cartoon /kɑːˈtuːn/
chat show /tʃæt ˌʃəʊ/ (US = talk show)
chat show host /ˈtʃæt ˌʃəʊ ˌhəʊst/
documentary /ˌdɒkjəˈmentəri/
game show /ˈgeɪm ˌʃəʊ/
newsreader /ˈnjuːzˌriːdə/ (US = newscaster)
presenter /prɪˈzentə/
the news /ðə ˈnjuːz/
soap opera /ˈsəʊpˌɒpərə/
viewer /ˈvjuːə/

## 12 Cinema

action film /ˈækʃən fɪlm/
actor /ˈæktə/ (can be used for a man or a woman)
actress /ˈæktrəs/ (some women prefer to be called *actor*)
animated film /ˌænɪmeɪtɪd ˈfɪlm/
cameraman /ˈkæmərəmæn/
comedy /ˈkɒmədi/
costume designer /ˈkɒstjuːm dɪˌzaɪnə/
director /dɪˈrektə/
film star /ˈfɪlm ˌstɑː/
horror film /ˈhɒrə ˌfɪlm/
make-up artist /ˈmeɪkʌp ˌɑːtɪst/
producer /prəˈdjuːsə/
science fiction film /ˌsaɪəns ˈfɪkʃən ˌfɪlm/
thriller /ˈθrɪlə/
war film /ˈwɔː ˌfɪlm/
western /ˈwestən/

## 13 Newspapers and magazines

article /ˈɑːtɪkl/
broadsheet /ˈbrɔːdʃiːt/
daily /ˈdeɪli/
editor /ˈedɪtə/
feature /ˈfiːtʃə/
headline /ˈhedlaɪn/
local newspaper /ˌləʊkəl ˈnjuːsˌpeɪpə/

national newspaper /ˌnæʃənəl ˈnjuːsˌpeɪpə/
paparazzi /ˌpæpərˈætsi/
the press /ðə ˈpres/
reporter /rɪˈpɔːtə/
tabloid /ˈtæblɔɪd/
weekly /ˈwiːkli/

## 14 Books

atlas /ˈætləs/
author /ˈɔːθə/
autobiography /ˌɔːtəbaɪˈɒgrəfi/
biography /baɪˈɒgrəfi/
chapter /ˈtʃæptə/
character /ˈkærəktə/
comic /ˈkɒmɪk/
computer manual /kəmˈpjuːtə ˌmænjuəl/
cookery book /ˈkʊkəri ˌbʊk/
dictionary /ˈdɪkʃənəri/
encyclopedia /ɪnˌsaɪkləˈpiːdiə/
guidebook /ˈgaɪdbʊk/
hardback /ˈhɑːdbæk/
novel /ˈnɒvəl/
paperback /ˈpeɪpəbæk/
textbook /ˈteksbʊk/
title /ˈtaɪtl/

## 15 Cooking

bake /beɪk/
boil /bɔɪl/
chop /tʃɒp/
fry /fraɪ/
grate /greɪt/
grill /grɪl/
peel /piːl/
roast /rəʊst/
slice /slaɪs/
spread /spred/ (*past tense* & *past participle* spread)
squeeze /skwiːz/

## 16 The taste of food

bitter /ˈbɪtə/
delicious /dɪˈlɪʃəs/
horrible /ˈhɒrəbl/
mild /maɪld/
rich /rɪtʃ/
salty /ˈsɔːlti/
sour /saʊə/
spicy /ˈspaɪsi/
sweet /swiːt/
tasteless /ˈteɪsləs/

## 17 Sounds

bang /bæŋ/
buzz /bʌz/
crackle /ˈkrækl/
creak /kriːk/
crunch /krʌnʃ/
fizz /fɪz/
pop /pɒp/
ring /rɪŋ/ (*past tense* rang, *past participle* rung)
sizzle /ˈsɪzl/
splash /splæʃ/

## 18 Home technology

burglar alarm /ˈbɜːglə əˌlɑːm/
CD player /ˌsiːˈdiː ˌpleɪə/
cordless phone /ˌkɔːdləs ˈfəʊn/
digital camera /ˌdɪdʒɪtəl ˈkæmərə/
DVD player /ˌdiːviːˈdiː ˌpleɪə/
minidisc player /ˈmɪnidɪsk ˌpleɪə/
radio-alarm clock /ˌreɪdiəʊ əˈlɑːm ˌklɒk/
remote control /rɪˌməʊt kənˈtrəʊl/
satellite dish /ˈsætəlaɪt ˌdɪʃ/
widescreen TV /ˌwaɪdskriːn ˌtiːˈviː/

## 19 The environment

acid rain /ˌæsɪd ˈreɪn/
exhaust fumes /ɪgˈzɔːst ˌfjuːmz/
global warming /ˌgləʊbəl ˈwɔːmɪŋ/
greenhouse effect /ˈgriːnhaʊs ɪˌfekt/
nuclear waste /ˌnjuːkliə ˈweɪst/
organic /ɔːˈgænɪk/
ozone layer /ˈəʊzəʊn ˌleɪə/
pesticides /ˈpestɪsaɪdz/
pollute /pəˈluːt/
pollution /pəˈluːʃən/
recycle /ˌriːˈsaɪkl/
recycling /ˌriːˈsaɪklɪŋ/

## 20 Natural disasters

avalanche /ˈævəlɑːnʃ/
casualties /ˈkæʒjuəltiz/
death toll /ˈdeθ ˌtəʊl/
drought /draʊt/
earthquake /ˈɜːθkweɪk/
flood /flʌd/
forest fire /ˌfɒrɪst ˈfaɪə/
hurricane /ˈhʌrɪkən/
rescue operation /ˈreskjuː ˌɒpərˌeɪʃən/
rescue workers /ˈreskjuː ˌwɜːkəz/
state of emergency /ˌsteɪt əv ɪˈmɜːdʒənsi/
survivors /səˈvaɪvəz/
victims /ˈvɪktɪmz/
volcanic eruption /vɒlˌkænɪk ɪˈrʌpʃən/

## 21 Studying at university

agriculture /ˈægrɪkʌltʃə/
architecture /ˈɑːkɪtektʃə/
business studies /ˈbɪznɪs ˌstʌdiz/
degree /dɪˈgriː/
engineering /ˌendʒɪˈnɪərɪŋ/
journalism /ˈdʒɜːnəlɪzəm/
law /lɔː/

lecture /ˈlektʃə/
lecturer /ˈlektʃərə/ (US = teacher or professor)
medicine /ˈmedsən/
modern languages /ˌmɒdən ˈlæŋgwɪdʒɪz/
politics /ˈpɒlətɪks/
seminar /ˈsemɪnɑː/
student /ˈstjuːdənt/

## 22 Crime

arrest /əˈrest/
break into /ˌbreɪk ˈɪntə/ (*past tense* broke, *past participle* broken)
burglar /ˈbɜːglə/
burglary /ˈbɜːgləri/
commit a crime /kəˌmɪt ə ˈkraɪm/
criminal /ˈkrɪmɪnəl/
murder /ˈmɜːdə/
murderer /ˈmɜːdərə/
shoplifter /ˈʃɒpˌlɪftə/
shoplifting /ˈʃɒplɪftɪŋ/
steal /stiːl/ (*past tense* stole, *past participle* stolen)
terrorism /ˈterərɪzəm/
terrorist /ˈterərɪst/
victim /ˈvɪktɪm/

## 23 Law and justice

court /kɔːt/
evidence /ˈevɪdəns/
guilty /ˈgɪlti/
innocent /ˈɪnəsənt/
judge /dʒʌdʒ/
jury /ˈdʒʊəri/
lawyer /ˈlɔɪə/ (US = attorney)
police /pəˈliːs/
prison /ˈprɪzən/
sentence /ˈsentəns/
witness /ˈwɪtnəs/

## 24 Getting a job

advertisement /əd'vɜːtɪsmənt/
application form /ˌæplɪ'keɪʃən ˌfɔːm/
apply /ə'plaɪ/
benefits /'benɪfɪts/
CV /ˌsiː'viː/ (curriculum vitae) (US = résumé)
experience /ɪk'spɪəriəns/
interview /'ɪntəvjuː/
pension /'penʃən/
qualifications /ˌkwɒlɪfɪ'keɪʃənz/
reference /'refərəns/
salary /'sæləri/
vacancy /'veɪkənsi/

## 25 Talking about your work

be made redundant /biː ˌmeɪd rɪ'dʌndənt/
be promoted /ˌbiː prə'məʊtɪd/
earning /'ɜːnɪŋ/
employed /ɪm'plɔɪd/
pay rise /'peɪ ˌraɪz/
permanent /'pɜːmənənt/
set up a business /ˌset ʌp ə 'bɪznɪs/ (*past tense* & *past participle* set)
temporary /'tempərəri/
the office /ðiː 'ɒfɪs/
training /'treɪnɪŋ/
unemployed /ˌʌnɪm'plɔɪd/
what do you do? /ˌwɒt duː juː 'duː/
work as /'wɜːk əz/
work for /'wɜːk fɔː/
work from home /ˌwɜːk frəm 'həʊm/
work in /'wɜːk ɪn/
work long hours /ˌwɜːk ˌlɒŋ 'aʊəz/

## 26 Who works in a company

accounts manager /ə'kaʊnts ˌmænɪdʒə/
boss /bɒs/
chief executive /ˌtʃiːf ɪg'zekjətɪv/
managing director /ˌmænɪdʒɪŋ daɪ'rektə/
personal assistant /ˌpɜːsənəl ə'sɪstənt/
personnel manager /ˌpɜːsən'el ˌmænɪdʒə/
receptionist /rɪ'sepʃənɪst/
sales manager /'seɪlz ˌmænɪdʒə/
sales representative /seɪlz ˌreprɪˌzentətɪv/
secretary /'sekrətəri/

## 27 Money

afford /ə'fɔːd/
bills /bɪlz/
expenses /ɪk'spensɪz/
interest /'ɪntrəst/
loss /lɒs/
mortgage /'mɔːgɪdʒ/
owe /əʊ/
poor /pɔː/
profit /'prɒfɪt/
rent /rent/
rich /rɪtʃ/
taxes /'tæksɪz/
wages /'weɪdʒɪz/

## 28 Using a computer

click on /ˌklɪk 'ɒn/
close /kləʊz/
copy /'kɒpi/
cut /kʌt/ (*past tense* & *past participle* cut)
delete /dɪ'liːt/
edit /'edɪt/
exit /'eksɪt/
highlight /'haɪlaɪt/
key /kiː/

open /'əʊpən/
paste /peɪst/
print /prɪnt/
save /seɪv/
scroll /skrəʊl/

## 29 Politics

be elected /biː ɪ'lektɪd/
be in power /biː ɪn 'paʊə/
candidate /'kændɪdət/
government /'gʌvənmənt/
hold an election /ˌhəʊld ən ɪ'lekʃən/ (*past tense* & *past participle* held)
minister /'mɪnɪstə/
policy /'pɒləsi/
political party /pəˌlɪtɪkəl 'pɑːti/
politician /ˌpɒlɪ'tɪʃən/
president /'prezɪdənt/
prime minister /ˌpraɪm 'mɪnɪstə/
vote for /'vəʊt ˌfɔː/

## 30 War and peace

ally /'ælaɪ/
army /'ɑːmi/
attack /ə'tæk/
capture /'kæptʃə/
ceasefire /'siːsfaɪə/
civilians /sɪ'vɪliənz/
declare /dɪ'kleə/
defend /dɪ'fend/
enemy /'enəmi/
invade /ɪn'veɪd/
peace talks /'piːs ˌtɔːks/
prisoners /'prɪzənəz/
retreat /rɪ'triːt/

## 31 Talking about language

accent /'æksənt/
adjective /'ædʒɪktɪv/
adverb /'ædvɜːb/
formal /'fɔːməl/
grammar /'græmə/
informal /ɪn'fɔːməl/
mean /miːn/ (*past tense* & *past participle* meant)
noun /naʊn/
pronounce /prə'naʊns/
pronunciation /prəˌnʌnsi'eɪʃən/
spell /spel/ (*past tense* & *past participle* spelt *or* spelled)
translate /trænz'leɪt/
verb /vɜːb/
vocabulary /və'kæbjələri/

## 32 Expressions of time

at last /ət 'lɑːst/
at once /ət 'wʌns/
at the moment /ət ðə 'məʊmənt/
for ages /fɔːr eɪdʒɪz/
from now on /frəm ˌnaʊ 'ɒn/
in time /ˌɪn 'taɪm/
no longer /ˌnəʊ 'lɒŋgə/
now and then /ˌnaʊ ən 'ðen/
on time /ˌɒn 'taɪm/
so far /ˌsəʊ 'fɑː/
these days /'ðiːz ˌdeɪz/

## 33 Everyday objects

brush /brʌʃ/
diary /'daɪəri/
keys /kiːz/
lighter /'laɪtə/
loose change /'luːs 'tʃeɪndʒ/
plasters /'plɑːstəz/

scissors /'sɪzəz/
tissues /'tɪʃuːz/
train timetable /'treɪn ˌtaɪmˌteɪbl/
umbrella /ʌm'brelə/

## 34 Household objects and tools

ashtray /'æʃˌtreɪ/
coat hanger /'kəʊt ˌhæŋə/
drill /drɪl/
hammer /'hæmə/
light bulb /'laɪt ˌbʌlb/
saw /sɔː/
screwdriver /'skruːˌdraɪvə/
tape measure /'teɪp ˌmeʒə/
tool /tuːl/
torch /tɔːtʃ/ (US = flashlight)
vase /vɑːz/

## 35 How good/bad something is

amusing /ə'mjuːzɪŋ/
awful /'ɔːfəl/
boring /'bɔːrɪŋ/
brilliant /'brɪliənt/
disappointing /ˌdɪsə'pɔɪntɪŋ/
dreadful /'dredfəl/
dull /dʌl/
enjoyable /ɪn'dʒɔɪəbl/
entertaining /ˌentə'teɪnɪŋ/
exciting /ɪk'saɪtɪŋ/
fascinating /'fæsɪneɪtɪŋ/
great /greɪt/
interesting /'ɪntrəstɪŋ/
terrible /'terəbl/
wonderful /'wʌndəfəl/

## 36 Describing objects

cardboard /ˈkɑːdbɔːd/
glass /glɑːs/
leather /ˈleðə/
made of /ˈmeɪd ɒv/
material /məˈtɪəriəl/
metal /ˈmetəl/
paper /ˈpeɪpə/
plastic /ˈplæstɪk/
rubber /ˈrʌbə/
stuff /stʌf/
thing /θɪŋ/
use for /ˈjuːs fə/
use to /ˈjuːs tə/
wood /wʊd/

## 37 Using your eyes

blink /blɪŋk/
examine /ɪgˈzæmɪn/
frown /fraʊn/
gaze /geɪz/
glance /glɑːns/
glare /gleə/
look at /ˈlʊk ət/
look for /ˈlʊk fə/
peep /piːp/
squint /skwɪnt/
stare /steə/
wink /wɪŋk/

## 38 Ways of walking

crawl /krɔːl/
creep /kriːp/ (*past tense* & *past participle* crept)
hop /hɒp/
limp /lɪmp/
march /mɑːtʃ/

paddle /'pædl/
skip /skɪp/
slip /slɪp/
stroll /strəʊl/
trip /trɪp/

## 39 Phrasal verbs

calm down /ˌkɑːm 'daʊn/
cheer up /ˌtʃɪə 'ʌp/
come on /ˌkʌm 'ɒn/ (*past tense* came, *past participle* come)
hang on /ˌhæŋ 'ɒn/ (*past tense* & *past participle* hung)
make up /ˌmeɪk 'ʌp/ (*past tense* & *past participle* made)
pick up /ˌpɪk 'ʌp/
put up with /ˌpʊt 'ʌp wɪð/ (*past tense* & *past participle* put)
slow down /ˌsləʊ 'daʊn/
speed up /ˌspiːd 'ʌp/
take up /ˌteɪk 'ʌp (*past tense* took, *past participle* taken)

## 40 Giving your opinion

as far as I'm concerned /əz fɑː əz 'aɪm kənˌsɜːnd/
I agree /aɪ ə'griː/
I believe in /aɪ bɪ'liːv ɪn/
I disagree /aɪ ˌdɪsə'griː/
I have my doubts about /aɪ hæv maɪ 'daʊts əˌbaʊt/
I'm against /aɪm ə'genst/
I'm in favour of /aɪm ɪn 'feɪvə əv/
in my opinion /ɪn 'maɪ əˌpɪnjən/
in my view /ɪn 'maɪ ˌvjuː/
I think /'aɪ ˌθɪŋk/
point of view /ˌpɔɪnt əv 'vjuː/
to my mind /təː 'maɪ ˌmaɪnd/
What do you think of … ? /ˌwɒt duː juː ˌθɪŋk əv/
What do you think about … ? /ˌwɒt duː juː ˌθɪŋk əˌbaʊt/

## Acknowledgements

I am very grateful to all the schools, institutions, teachers and students around the world who either piloted or commented on the material:

Katie Head, Cambridge, UK
Tadeusz Wolanski, Gdansk, Poland

I am also grateful to staff and students at the following institutions who tested the pilot material:

British Language Training Centre, Amsterdam, Netherlands
EPFC, Brussels, Belgium
Mercator-PCVD, Gent, Belgium
Sint Andreasinstitut, Bruges, Belgium

I would particularly like to thank Nóirín Burke and Martine Walsh at Cambridge University Press for all their help, guidance and support during the writing of this series. My thanks also to Liz Driscoll for her experienced editing of the material and to Jo Barker and Sarah Warburton for their excellent design and artwork.